All
Christians
Are
Charismatic

The Bible for Christian Life

In Between Advents
Dennis E. Groh

The Work of God Goes On
Gerhard Lohfink

All Christians Are Charismatic
Lowell J. Satre

All Christians Are Charismatic

Sharing Faith, Fruit, Charisms

Lowell J. Satre

THE BIBLE FOR CHRISTIAN LIFE

FORTRESS PRESS   PHILADELPHIA

To Elizabeth

Gifted, giving gift from God

Library of Congress Cataloging-in-Publication Data

Satre, Lowell J.
  All Christians are charismatic.

  (The Bible for Christian Life)
  Bibliography: p.
  1. Gifts, Spiritual. I. Title. II. Series.
  BT767.3.S28 1988   234'.13   87–45902
  ISBN 0-8006-2023-2

3210H87   Printed in the United States of America   1–2023

Contents

Preface

Since the early 1960s, I have been involved officially and unofficially in observing the beginnings and growth of the neo-Pentecostal movement.

Through the years I have been a party to extended conversations with many a person perplexed by, aghast at, dead set against, or enthusiastic about speaking in tongues. For some time I have taught an elective course at Luther Northwestern Theological Seminary, in St. Paul, usually under the title "The Fruit of the Spirit and the Gifts of Grace."

My experiences have prompted me to delve into the Scriptures, especially the New Testament, to find out what is taught there about God's Holy Spirit and the gifts of the Spirit. What I write is of course written from my perspective as a Lutheran Christian; I have no desire to escape my theological skin even if I could. Since every Christian has some spiritual gift and no individual believer has them all, I am perhaps as well qualified as the next member of Christ's body to share the results of study and experience related to charismatic gifts.

Urged on me by colleagues, former students, and others, this book has been made possible in large part by the sabbatical program of our seminary and by a grant awarded me by the Aid Association for Lutherans for the academic year 1977–78. There are many fine works on the Holy Spirit and charismatic gifts, some of which are much more comprehensive and exhaustive. This volume deals with some of the facts about the Holy Spirit that are most commonly and troublesomely misunderstood. More particularly, to bring order to the welter of New Testament terms used by proponents, opponents, and exponents of the neo-Pentecostal movement, the book vigorously proposes that we all agree on a basic principle: that of using such terms in accordance with the way they, or their roots or derivatives, are used in the New Testament. Since all parties to the contemporary discussion profoundly respect Scripture, it would seem that this principle might be an obvious and acceptable one. Evidence from the Book of Acts is important, as is that from the New Testament generally, especially from Paul, who wrote earliest and with firsthand knowledge. It is not least among Lutherans, so historically and openly committed to the Scriptures as the sole authority for faith and life, that this proposal should be eagerly embraced.

Among the words and phrases to be discussed are "charismatic," "the free gift of God," "faith," "to baptize with the Holy Spirit," "to be filled with the Holy Spirit," "full of the Holy Spirit," "the kingdom's coming with power," "infant baptism," "the fruit of the Spirit," "spiritual gifts," "the charismatic congregation."

This is no mere word battle but a crisis in vocabulary that involves fundamentals and continues to disturb individuals and congregations of many denominations, both their lay members and their pastors. In this crisis the opportunities seem to outweigh the dangers more than at any other time in the past fifteen years. Generally speaking, all Christians— leaders of renewal movements, church officials, clergy, lay persons, and theologians—are considerably less shrill and more open to dialogue and mutual understanding than they were in the sixties. On the one hand, the positive results of an emphasis on spiritual gifts are more widely accepted; on the other hand, there seems to be a desire on all sides that such an emphasis be positively and honestly related to the Scriptures and the historic Christian confessions.

The author will be most blessed if even one person can confidently affirm from perusing this book, "In Christ, all things are mine and I am Christ's; as a Christian, I am charismatic, freely gifted by the 'Spirit, who apportions to each one individually as the Spirit wills.' "

1

All Christians Are Charismatic

A Gifted People

According to some, John F. Kennedy was, Lyndon Johnson was not; Nelson Rockefeller was, Dwight D. Eisenhower was not. Was what? Charismatic, of course. The adjective is used in common speech to describe those capable of stirring popular support and enthusiasm, although their actual accomplishments may be less than that of leaders lacking such charisma.

Another legitimate use of the adjective is to describe Christians who specially emphasize the significance of the charismata or charisms—free gifts from God's Spirit such as those mentioned in 1 Corinthians 12, Romans 12, and Ephesians 4. And often their particular emphasis is on such gifts as healing, prophecy, and speaking in tongues. This is not at all to say that Christians who are charismatic in this sense neglect other aspects of Christian faith and life. In fact, their aim generally is so to live in the Holy Spirit as to proclaim that Jesus is Lord to the glory of God the Father: wholeheartedly they identify with the gospel and mission of the early church. But many if not most of these Christians hold that speaking in tongues is a common if not indispensable experience of those who have been baptized in the Holy Spirit.

There is a third way in which the adjective is coming to be used more and more in the church, by both Protestants and Catholics. It is in a sense that is most closely related to the meanings of the New Testament Greek words from which "charismatic" is derived. In the New Testament generally, *charisma* is a "free gift" given by the God who shows *charis,* that is, grace or undeserved favor, to people. No one can earn either grace or the free gift of grace. Death can be earned, a free gift cannot: "For the wages of sin is death, but the free gift [*charisma*] of God is eternal life in Christ Jesus our Lord" (Rom. 6:23). By definition, grace is absolutely free, not for sale: "No one can have it for anything, yet anyone may have it for nothing."

"Charismatic," then, according to its New Testament Greek roots means "gifted." For the New Testament, the charismatic is the graciously, freely, undeservedly gifted by God. Among Christians, ought this not therefore to be the primary and proper meaning of "charismatic"? It is not possible, of course, to exclude popular and secondary meanings of the word, but the understanding among Christians might be enhanced if we agreed to keep the primary meaning to the fore.

Every Christian is grace-gifted—and how gifted! "The free gift of God is eternal life." This gift is fundamental.

Our God is love. God cares enough for you and me and all the world of people to give God's only Son, who embodies the love of Father and Son. "To him who loves us and has freed us from our sins by his blood and made us a kingdom, priests to his God and Father, to him be glory and dominion for ever and ever. Amen" (Rev. 1:5-6). Knowing God as his own loving Father, Jesus mediated God's unconditional caring for sinners to those he met. "Just exactly as you are, God loves you" was a message that warmed and pulled people to him, especially notorious sinners. God's actively caring heart in Jesus reaches out for all through the parable of the father waiting for his wandering son, who is poignantly missed and longed-for throughout the time he is gone from home. When he returns, his father spots him far away and sprints to embrace, forgive, and restore the beloved son (Luke 15:11-24).

Forgiveness—that is the primary reality that eternal life is about! Before God, everyone apart from Christ is guilty. In Christ, God pronounces an absolution on the whole world, "not counting their trespasses against them" (2 Cor. 5:19). God has decreed forgiveness through the crucified and risen Christ: those who believe in forgiveness have it, as Luther was fond of saying.

God's free gift of eternal life is essentially faith, knowing God experientially in Jesus Christ: "And this is eternal life, that they know thee the only true God, and Jesus Christ whom thou hast sent" (John 17:3).

Life eternal belongs to the ages: the believer lives abundantly both now and after death. This is our hope, which is faith facing the future. "Faith, hope, love *abide*" (1 Cor. 13:13). Eternity cannot exhaust God's loving promises nor the lively surprises in Christ for those who trust God!

The Indispensable Spirit

Without the Holy Spirit, eternal life is null and void. The Spirit is the indispensable One who convinces the world of sin and righteousness and judgment. Pentecost was a new beginning for the Twelve. During Jesus' earthly ministry, the Father had revealed to them that Jesus was the *Christ,* and after his death they had seen the risen Jesus. But the *meaning* of his resurrection (Lazarus and others regained life!), that Jesus Christ is *Lord,* was not driven home to them till God through Jesus gave the Spirit on Pentecost (Acts 2:33). Then Peter could herald with conviction, "Let all the house of Israel therefore know assuredly that God has made him both Lord and Christ, this Jesus whom you crucified" (Acts 2:36). "No one can say 'Jesus is Lord' except by the Holy Spirit" (1 Cor. 12:3).

In the charismatic life of every Christian, then, the free gift (*charisma*) of eternal life, consisting of faith in Jesus as Lord, is the beginning, middle, and end. It need never end, however. Having planted faith through the gospel, God's Holy Spirit of Jesus continues working in the believer in another way: the Spirit produces fruit. "The fruit of the Spirit is love, joy, peace, patience, kindness, goodness, faithfulness, gentleness, self-control" (Gal. 5:22–23). "The fruit of the Spirit *is* love," and it is "the fruit of the *Spirit*." The Spirit is the producer, not we. This gracious gifting is for every Christian: all Christians are charismatic!

Some years ago, a primary-school teacher began to experience a sharp pain in her right thumb, hindering greatly the use of her hand for her daily activities of cutting with scissors, writing, and drawing. Consulting her health maintenance organization, she was told the muscles of her right thumb were atrophying and was advised to go to a local hospital for X-rays and further consultation. There the original diagnosis was confirmed by two specialists. Although no cure was suggested, she was given a few pain pills. When they ran out, she got no others.

The pain persisted, becoming even more severe, especially at night, when it would usually awaken her several times. She knew the Lord Christ could remove her affliction, but he evidently did not see fit to do so although in faith she and others prayed for this more than once.

One morning she must have mentioned her suffering of the preceding night to her son, who was living at home. That evening before he left for a prayer meeting of young people at a church near a state university, he said rather casually, "Mom, I'm going to ask my prayer group tonight to pray that your thumb be healed."

Several days, maybe a week, later the teacher realized with a start that her thumb pained her no more, nor did she experience any difficulty in her usual activities, in the classroom or out! She hesitated to mention it immediately, lest her relief be merely temporary. But after a time, she told her husband and her son. Could it be that the Lord had done this especially to encourage her son's faith? At any rate, she knew her healing was a charism, an act of God's sheer grace. During more than a decade with a healthy, perfectly functioning pair of thumbs, she has thanked God many times for healing mercy, confident also that God's grace is enough should the affliction recur.

Sam and Verna were awaiting eagerly the birth of their first child, as were both of their families. Suddenly tiny Monica arrived, pronounced perfect after a superficial examination in the delivery room. Sam notified his parents and others of the momentous event. Then, abruptly, things changed. Monica was rushed to a children's hospital for radical surgery necessary for her survival. The surgery was successful; but the half has not been told. That first day Sam and Verna were informed of symptoms that pointed to the extent of the difficulties facing the five-pound, fourteen-ounce Monica. Even before the results of the chromosome tests were in, both parents and attending pediatrician were ninety-five percent certain that little Monica was a Down's-syndrome child.

In the intervening months the parents went through feelings of rebellion, anger, frustration, and disappointment, and they shed many tears. There may be more ahead. But the Lord's tough grace seems to be winning this battle. God's Spirit is producing love, joy, peace, and patience—in parents, two sets of grandparents, uncles, and aunts, the whole clan, and in numerous sensitive neighbors and friends. Doctors have been skillful and considerate, the nurses helpful, even compassionate. Verna and Sam's pastor visited at the right time with appropriate words of strength, hope, and challenge, including this word: "Verna, it's your job to get this little baby ready for heaven." Soon after, Monica was baptized into the death and resurrection of Christ. The pastor announced that a new little sister had been welcomed into the people of God. Congregation, neighborhood, relatives, and friends have all rallied with depth and warmth. New vistas for service have beckoned in light of the experience.

Early on, Monica became a tiny "eight o'clock scholar," lovingly called for each morning and returned toward noon in a van provided by her city's social services. At her school, Monica is gently and firmly drawn and pushed each day toward realizing the utmost of her potential. Parents, grandparents, and others also work and play at this. God's grace is proving enough and more than enough for all concerned, who have ties now they never had before with a significant portion of God's people. Although they did not express it in the words of former Senator Hubert Humphrey, whose first granddaughter was a Down's-syndrome child, they nevertheless could empathize with his feelings. "Why us?" he questioned. "We couldn't understand why. But out of that experience came a whole new set of values for our family. This little girl taught us more love than all the Sunday school teaching I've had. I began to really understand what it means to love and be loved."[1]

These two incidents, the teacher's healing and the loving acceptance of a handicapped infant, are put back to back because they point to God's giving grace-gifts, charisms, to God's children. In the one instance God gave the gift of healing, in the other the gift of grace that enabled Monica's parents and others to welcome her and to keep loving and caring for her with joy, sometimes joy *and* tears. God's grace suffices. To put this another way: Paul was charismatic when he taught, exhorted, and healed. He was also charismatic when three times the Lord said no to his prayer for release from his own thorn in the flesh. But the Lord promised, "My grace [*charis*] is enough for you, for my power is consummated in weakness" (2 Cor. 12:9, au. trans.).

The Grace of Christ

Jesus was and is God's grace in human form. His visible, earthly life ended on a cross, the most characteristic expression of God's grace. Christ, charism, and cross—in God's economy in this end time, these

belong together. Since suffering for Christ's sake is as much God's gift
as is the gift of healing, Paul could write from jail, "For it has been
graciously given [*charizesthai*, a sister word of *charis*] you that for the
sake of Christ you should not only believe in him but also suffer for
him, engaging in the same fight that you saw and now hear to be mine"
(Phil. 1:29–30, au. trans.). As Jesus' life is characterized by the cross,
so is that of his disciple: "If any man would come after me, let him
deny himself and take up his cross and follow me" (Mark 8:34, par.
Matt. 16:24; cf. Luke 9:23 for "daily" crossbearing).

Yet the difficulty of crossbearing is undergirded by joy—deep, per-
sistent joy. It begins with the Spirit of the forerunner and foundation
of our faith, Jesus, "who for the joy that was set before him endured
the cross, despising the shame, and is seated at the right hand of the
throne of God" (Heb. 12:2). Since there is always joy in him, we
respond with enthusiasm when Paul invites us to "rejoice in the Lord
always; again I will say, Rejoice" (Phil. 4:4). Such responses may arise
in a hushed hospital room, a lonely prison cell, in the praises and
prayers of a great congregation, or in any group of believers. The joy
of Christians caring for one another has been a trademark from the
church's beginning. The earliest church chose to have "all things in
common. . . . And day by day, attending the temple together and breaking bread in their homes, they partook of food with glad and generous
hearts, praising God and having favor with all the people" (Acts
2:44–47).

Through the centuries one of the most significant aspects of God's
ongoing renewal of God's people is that deeply concerned small groups
of Christians arise. The importance of these agents of renewal for
church and community can scarcely be overestimated. Can a vital and
vibrant life in Christ be sustained by spending only one out of the 168
hours of the week in gatherings praising God, one hour that includes
a fifteen- to twenty-five-minute sermon? Perhaps so. But it would be
unlikely unless those involved had rich personal or family devotional
lives centered in the gospel and prayer. Wherever on earth two or three
or more are met in Christ's name (Matt. 18:20), there is the Lord in
the midst of the church through the same Spirit who provides in each
a mutual concern, a shared joy, and a reaching-out for the lost. This
relational dimension of congregational life, which the church in general
has "loved long since and lost awhile," may be the most significant and

lasting contribution of the neo-Pentecostal movement of our day. In first century "house churches" and in later groups of Christians gathered for Bible study, prayer, and the seeking of God's will, renewal has often broken out in the church to leaven the community's moral, social, political, economic, and educational life. Renewal broke forth in early Rome, in eighteenth-century Germany and England, in nineteenth-century Norway, and in many other times and places. Both distinguished anthropologists and eminent church leaders see in the small group an indispensable factor in the rapid expansion of neo-Pentecostal Christianity, whether within the churches or in breaking new ground.

Today, there are various kinds of renewal movements that tend to exclude some Christians. We have, for example, liturgical renewal, evangelical renewal, charismatic renewal, and so on. Throughout the church catholic there need be no fencing out. Renewal has been a part of the Christian church since its beginning, and of Christians in the United States since long before the last two decades. Renewal need not come about in an exclusive way. As there is almost an infinite variety in human beings, such is the variety in which the Holy Spirit renews.

Almost sixty years ago a rural congregation in Iowa held a series of "evangelistic meetings." After the lay evangelist's law-gospel sermon one evening, opportunity was given for testimonies. When some in the gathering had stood up to witness to God's grace, there arose a man whose heart had been "strangely warmed" by the preaching of Christ that week. Baptized and confirmed in a nearby country church, he felt that something—rather, Someone—had powerfully gripped him that night, and he would say so. For what seemed like an hour but was probably two minutes, he just stood there in tears; usually articulate, he could speak not a word. Whether he was renewed or converted, only God knows, who alone knows the heart. But in that man's life there was a profound change that lasted through his death over forty years later.

Does this man's experience prove that when God's Spirit renews or converts a person, that person becomes momentarily tongue-tied? It is as ridiculous to say that every time God touches or fills one with the Holy Spirit, one's tongue is loosed into confession or glossolalia or testimony! "Not all are apostles nor prophets nor teachers, are they? Not all work miracles nor possess the gifts of healing, do they? Not all speak in tongues nor interpret them, do they?" (1 Cor. 12:29–30, au. trans.). Some do—but not all. Nevertheless, *Christians are charismatic,* for each has the charism of eternal life, that is, faith; "all were baptized in one Spirit" (1 Cor. 12:13, au. trans.); all have the fruit of the Spirit; and to each is given a charism for the congregation: "the manifestation of the Spirit for the common good" (1 Cor. 12:7).

If we agree on this, there will be more openness to a catholic kerygmatic renewal that heralds with one voice the kerygma "that Jesus Christ is Lord, to the glory of God the Father" (Phil. 2:11).

2

The Spirit's Indispensable Gift

What is the indispensable gift from God's Spirit? What is that without which there is nothing? Is it the gift of wisdom, of knowledge, of healing? Could it be the gift of tongues, of administration, of teaching? Which of these is indispensable, or is it none of these?

A Priceless Treasure

Jesus' life, crucifixion, and resurrection constitute the core of our confession. When Jesus walked our planet visibly, he soon became offensive to most people of repute because he had table fellowship with notorious sinners. Imagine what would happen today if you or I should invite a drug pusher or a prostitute home to dinner. "This fellow welcomes sinners and feasts with them" (Luke 15:2, au. trans.) was the word with which his enemies unintentionally glorified him. This word is followed in Luke by the parables of the lost sheep, the lost coin, and the two lost sons. The waiting father races to embrace his returning son, just as he was. In Simon's house, Jesus accepted anointing, trust, and love from a "woman of the city, who was a sinner"; he forgave her and pronounced her whole. Passing through Jericho, he invited himself to spend the day with Zacchaeus, dishonest as he was. The poor had "good news preached to them" by Jesus (Matt. 11:5) and became persuaded that God is as gracious as Jesus; he said to a fearful, faithful, hemorrhaging woman, "Courage, daughter, your faith has made you whole" (Matt. 9:22, au. trans.).

Ministering in this manner around Galilee, Jesus evoked an upsurge of faith, primarily among the poor, those who were generally looked down upon. Their "looking sad" at Jesus' death is easily understood: "We had hoped he was the one to redeem Israel" (Luke 24:21). Although some Israelites had believed him to be the Messiah, others conspired with the Romans to have him crucified under Pontius Pilate as an impostor. Having buried him, they made the sepulcher "secure" by a sealed stone. But he could not be boxed in: all heaven broke loose and Jesus was around again, looking different yet still the same, dropping in on his friends and inspiring their renewed trust.

The earliest witnesses to the resurrected Jesus were not so much interested in who Jesus was as in who he *is!* Who he is becomes evident only as the Spirit of the risen, glorified Jesus persuades people who he is *for them.* In the language of the Fourth Gospel the crucifixion is his glorification. The content of this Spirit-inspired, resurrection faith shines through at a number of points in the New Testament. Listen to Peter on Pentecost: "God has made him both Lord and Christ, this Jesus whom you crucified" (Acts 2:36). Hear the resurrection confession of Paul in Romans: "If you confess with your lips that Jesus is Lord and believe in your heart that God raised him from the dead, you will be saved" (Rom. 10:9).

In his first letter to Corinth, Paul concluded his brief introduction to spiritual gifts by remarking, "No one speaking by the Spirit of God ever says 'Jesus be cursed!' and no one can say 'Jesus is Lord' except by the Holy Spirit" (1 Cor. 12:3). In a context intended primarily to state what spiritual gifts are not, Paul stated that it is only by the Holy Spirit that one can confess, "Jesus is Lord."

The indispensable gift of God's Spirit, then, is faith, a faith that confesses, "Jesus Christ crucified and risen is my Lord." This faith is "God's gift of eternal life" (Rom. 6:23). Faith is life eternal, in the sense that it is, qualitatively, genuine life, "life that is life indeed." This passage from Romans points also to the never-ending aspect of this "life abundant."

That a crucified Jew affords the only way in which God saves is incredible: "I believe that I cannot by my own understanding or effort believe in Jesus Christ my Lord or come to him. But the Holy Spirit has called me through the Gospel" (Luther, Small Catechism). The Holy Spirit makes the incredible credible. Therefore, I believe!

The Good News

God's indispensable gift is given through the gospel. The content of faith and that of the gospel are identical: Jesus crucified, risen, present, all for you and me. Paul summarized this Gospel as the "word of the cross." On that tree on Calvary, salvation was created. The resurrection was God's amen to the crucifixion, and the Spirit of Jesus alive comforts us in the gospel. Luther describes faith as a certain trust in God in which Christ is present. As Christ is present in the gospel preached, so he inhabits the gospel believed. We are saved not by faith in Christ but by Christ in faith—"through faith because of Christ."

The preaching of the gospel thus takes on exalted significance. "How are they to hear without a preacher?" (Rom. 10:14). "Great indeed, we confess, is the mystery of our religion:

> He was manifested in the flesh, vindicated in the Spirit, seen by angels, preached among the nations, believed on in the world, taken up in glory." (1 Tim. 3:16)

Preaching ranks right up there with incarnation, resurrection, ascension—and faith! Preaching is not to be defined as that which is proclaimed from the pulpit only. The gospel can be authentically communicated at work, or while washing dishes, or on a plane or bus—where not? But there will be no trust in the crucified One unless the word of the cross is first heard.

Baptism is included in that gospel. On the road from Jerusalem to Gaza, Philip the evangelist heard an Ethiopian reading Isaiah 53 in his chariot. Invited aboard, Philip was asked what it meant. "Beginning with this scripture he told him the good news of Jesus. And . . . as they came to some water, . . . the eunuch said, 'See, here is water! What is to prevent my being baptized?' " (Acts 8:35–36). Since nothing prevented, Philip baptized him. From the evidence, Philip's good news of Jesus included the good news of baptism.

Peter's Pentecost proclamation also includes baptism (Acts 2:38–41): "So those who received his word were baptized." After the earthquake at Philippi, the jailer was open to the gospel. Paul and Silas "spoke the word of the Lord to him and to all that were in his house. And he . . . washed their wounds, and he was baptized at once, with all his family

. . .; and he rejoiced with all his household that he had believed in God" (Acts 16:32–34).

Since "households" include children according to ancient Greek usage and the language of both the Old Testament and early Christianity outside the New Testament, it is likely children are meant to be included in the several New Testament passages that tell of whole households being baptized. But this can be neither proved nor disproved! We do know from the church father Tertullian that infant baptism was practiced in northern Africa about A.D. 200. Not many years later Origen of Alexandria wrote that the church had received from the apostles the tradition to administer baptism to the very little ones also. When Gentiles converted to Judaism, proselyte baptism was administered to parents and children alike, including infants. This as well as the Jewish practice of circumcising on the eighth day might have helped influence the earliest church to baptize infants. It is likely but not certain.

Did Jesus want little children to be baptized? Although there is no direct evidence on this question, we may be able to detect the thinking of the church of the latter half of the first century, when Mark, Luke-Acts, and Matthew were written. In several passages there are clues to a very early baptismal liturgy containing a Greek verb variously translated "hinder," "prevent," or "forbid" (cf. Acts 8:36 above). "Can anyone forbid water for baptizing?" (Acts 10:47). "Then Jesus came from Galilee to the Jordan to John, to be baptized by him. John would have prevented him, saying, 'I need to be baptized by you, and do you come to me?' " (Matt. 3:13–14). This word for "prevent" or "hinder" is the same verb used in Mark 10:13–16, which tells of Jesus' indignation when the disciples rebuked those who brought children to him to touch. To his disciples Jesus said, "Let the children come to me, do not hinder them; for to such belongs the kingdom of God."

The question of infant baptism was likely not one of Jesus' time but arose when the gospel tradition was already in place. Those who handed on this story of Jesus blessing the children wanted Christians of their time to remember an occurrence by which they might solve the question. If this is true, we can understand that this story was transmitted in such a way that an early baptismal formula shines through it![2]

Yet we baptize infants primarily for theological reasons, not merely because the early church probably did. We believe that in baptism the living God bestows the Holy Spirit and the free gift of eternal life in Christ Jesus on the infant who is baptized in the water with the Word. What happens is rather like what happened to little Sam.

God gave Jake and Liz a daughter and a son of whom they were the biological parents. For various reasons they longed for another child. Since Liz had been advised by a physician for reasons of health not to bear another baby, they decided to adopt a child. After a considerable time, the adoption agency called to say they had a fine baby boy who they were convinced should be a part of Jake and Liz's family. Excitedly, mother and father, son and daughter went a short time later to see and bring home baby Sam! Not long afterwards in the county court, a judge declared Samuel to be the son of Liz and Jake, and it was duly recorded. It stands recorded! But little Sam knew nothing of all these heavy legal proceedings. Did that make them null and void? Absolutely not!

In Christ, God made the first move toward humankind, "reconciling the world to himself, not counting their trespasses against them." Toward an adult, God's Spirit makes the first move with the good news of Jesus that includes baptism. The response God's gospel seeks and elicits is faith and baptism. Toward an infant, the Spirit of God makes the first move in Christ's promise wet with the water of baptism and alive with the Spirit. As baptized children grow and are taught their identity in Christ by parents, siblings, pastor, and others, they come to *realize* who they are. But this relationship to God through baptism is real, long before one realizes one has been adopted through water and God's Word.

In the New Testament as a whole, there are joined together four realities dealing with the beginning of the Christian life; we tear them asunder at our peril. These four are the Spirit of Christ, the gospel of Christ, a right relationship to Christ, and baptism into Christ. Through the gospel of Christ, the Spirit persuades the adult hearer to believe in Christ and be baptized. Thus incorporated into Christ by the Spirit, the infant grows up into conscious faith, from faith to faith, in Christ. This is true whether the faith develops gradually or by a sudden recognition of the heritage provided by the person's "adoption papers." Wherever a Christian life begins, Spirit, gospel, baptism, and right relationship to Christ are there like the four sides of a square. Once in Acts it is reported that the Holy Spirit was given shortly after baptism (8:12–17), and on another occasion immediately before (10:44–48); the New Testament in general keeps the four realities closely together. From Pentecost onward, one reality does not normally appear without the others.

To be baptized in the name of the Trinity is "to be baptized in the Holy Spirit," whether or not the baptized is an infant. And since in the New Testament the experience of "being baptized in the Spirit" is always joined with God's initial, once-for-all baptizing, it is a source of great confusion for many Lutherans and other Christians when the phrase "baptism in the Spirit" is equated with God's subsequent filling or renewing in the Spirit, which is sometimes accompanied by speaking in tongues or prophecy. God *does* fill and renew in the Spirit after baptism, and prophecy and tongues *are* charisms of the Spirit; but why confuse the language of classical Pentecostalism with that of historic Lutheranism?

Wedded to the Word and the water for baptized believers is their sharing in the Lord's Table, by which they "proclaim the Lord's death until he comes." On Pentecost in Jerusalem "those who received [Peter's] word were baptized, and . . . devoted themselves to the apostles' teaching and fellowship, to the breaking of bread and the prayers" (Acts 2:41–42). From the earliest days Christian congregations have found that ancient prayers are often more modern than tomorrow, that liturgy and spontaneity well supplement each other.

The Spirit's indispensable gift, then, is faith in God's Messiah, Jesus. Other gifts from the Spirit are important, very important, yet no one of them is *indispensable* for an individual Christian. Faith is.

3

All Christians Are Given the Spirit

The Identity of the Gift

There is One who holds myriads of Milky Ways "in his hand," as the spiritual says, who watches as well a wee sparrow flying or fallen—all creatures great and small, including you and me. God is Creator and Lord of the Covenant, both the New and the Old.

It is basic to acknowledge the Holy Spirit as God, for the Holy Spirit is the Spirit of God the Creator and of the covenant God of Abraham, David, Mary, and John the Baptist. It is none other than the Spirit of the God of Jesus and his church, which is the "Israel of God." Of parallel importance is that the Holy Spirit is the Spirit of Messiah Jesus of Nazareth, who was crucified, died, and was buried, and is now risen, ascended Lord, still present with God's own through the same Spirit.

The Spirit that we Christians know *was* before Jesus' birth, in fact, from eternity. The Spirit "was not yet" (John 7:39, au. trans.) as we know it, however, till the risen Jesus gave the Holy Spirit to the church and to the world.

Always when you think of the Spirit, think of Jesus. That is whom the Spirit is all about. The Spirit is not isolated someplace doing something on its own; the Spirit *is* in order to witness to and glorify Jesus. The Holy Spirit's significance, therefore, cannot be overestimated.

The Gift of God's Spirit to Jesus

At the beginning of his public ministry, Jesus was baptized in the Jordan River by John the Baptist. The Holy Spirit descended upon him, and the Father's voice from heaven addressed him as beloved Son, implying his impending suffering on behalf of others. All four Gospels testify that this is the Servant Son of God, poised to fulfill cosmic and world history.

Full of the Spirit, Jesus was led up by the Spirit to be tempted by the devil. In the power of the Spirit, Jesus came to his hometown synagogue and made a bold claim in harmony with his Father's voice from heaven: "The Spirit of the Lord is upon me, because he has anointed me to preach good news to the poor" (Luke 4:18). The listeners at Nazareth became instant earwitnesses of the fulfillment of Isaiah's prophecy, for Jesus said, "Today this scripture has been fulfilled in your hearing" (Luke 4:21). In Jesus, instant kingdom of God!

By submitting to John's baptism, Jesus aligned himself with the Baptist's movement heralding the last age, the eschaton. It was the beginning of the end.

Spirit Baptism?

It is Jesus who baptizes in the Holy Spirit. There has been much said and written these last years about the "baptism of the Holy Spirit." The phrase suggests that the Holy Spirit is baptizing. How many times do you think the phrase "the baptism of the Holy Spirit" occurs in Scripture? Not even once! But six times the Gospels and Acts use the expression "baptize in the Holy Spirit" with Jesus as the baptizer. It is *Jesus* who baptizes in or with the Holy Spirit.

In Matthew, Mark, and Luke, John the Baptist is quoted as saying essentially these words to those confessing their sins: "I baptize you with water, but he who comes after me will baptize you with the Holy Spirit" (Matt. 3:11; Mark 1:7; Luke 3:16). In the Fourth Gospel, the Baptist says that the One who commissioned him to baptize with water said to him, "He on whom you see the Spirit descend and remain, this is he who baptizes with the Holy Spirit" (1:33). Jesus the Baptizer baptizes with the Holy Spirit—still today.

John's baptizing ceased. Before his ascension Jesus reminded his disciples that his baptizing was about to start: "John baptized with water, but before many days you shall be baptized with the Holy Spirit" (Acts 1:5). The other reference in Acts to Jesus' baptizing is in the context of Christianity's breakthrough to the Gentiles in Caesarea

(Acts 10—11). In his Jerusalem defense of his preaching and baptizing in the home of the Roman centurion Cornelius, who with his household was "granted repentance unto life" and the "gift of the Holy Spirit," Peter reminded his hearers how the Lord had said, "John baptized with water, but you shall be baptized with the Holy Spirit" (Acts 11:16). Since Pentecost, Jesus has never ceased baptizing with the Holy Spirit. Oh, he uses a poor stick of a preacher, to paraphrase Luther, but it is ultimately God who baptizes each with the Spirit of Jesus.

Years before the four Gospels and the Book of Acts were written, Paul wrote a letter to the gifted, contentious, proud Christians at Corinth. Some of the Corinthians considered themselves to be superspiritual because of their more spectacular gifts and knowledge. Christ's apostle would have none of this. He would not even call them spiritual. Instead he called them fleshly, because they were jealous, fighting like ordinary people. According to Paul, there are no Christians who have not been baptized in the Spirit. There are differences in spiritual gifts, yes! But are some baptized in the Holy Spirit and others not? No! Paul writes, "For in one Spirit we were all baptized into one body—Jews or Greeks, slaves or free—and we were all made to drink of one Spirit" (1 Cor. 12:13, au. trans.). The picture presented in this verse has Jesus or the Father baptizing in the Spirit into Christ's body, and God causing all to drink of the Spirit of Christ. *Tremendous diversity* coexists with *absolute unity*—all are baptized in one Spirit into one body!

The seven passages I have cited, from the Gospels, Acts, and 1 Corinthians, are the only places where the expression "baptized in the (Holy) Spirit" is used in the New Testament. Six out of seven times it is Jesus who baptizes in the Holy Spirit. In the seventh instance Jesus or the Father is the agent.

Has your baptism ever been called a mere "water baptism," perhaps by one who scoffed at the baptism of infants? If so, you were probably hurt by this attitude, even if God's love has long since healed the hurt. It can be admitted that there actually was a period of water baptism. John's pre-Christian baptism was simply water baptism because it occurred prior to Pentecost. But from Pentecost on, there was normally no such thing as mere water baptism. Christians baptize with water *and the Holy Spirit.*

God Gives to All

God's gift of the Holy Spirit is intended for all people. Was anyone left out in God's plan of salvation? Absolutely not! According to Luke, Peter on Pentecost quoted Joel: "And in the last days it shall be, God declares, that I will pour out my Spirit upon all flesh. . . . And it shall be that whoever calls on the name of the Lord shall be saved" (Acts 2:17, 21). God loves and acts on behalf of all God's children. "In Christ God was reconciling the world to himself, not counting their sins against them" (2 Cor. 5:19). The world was reconciled, not one person forgotten! After Peter's Pentecost sermon, his hearers asked, "What shall we do?" Did Peter say, "You can't do a thing"? God forbid! Peter replied, "Repent and be baptized every one of you in the name of Jesus Christ for the forgiveness of your sins; and you shall receive the gift of the Holy Spirit. . . . So those who received his word were baptized" (Acts 2:37–38, 41). God intends repentance, faith in Christ, baptism, and the gift that is the Holy Spirit for every person.

As we have seen, baptism in the Spirit happened to Paul and *all* his Corinthian readers (1 Cor. 12:13). To be baptized in the Spirit is not the mark of an elite; it is the initiatory experience common to *all* sinners trusting Christ who are baptized into him. In this verse of 1 Corinthians, the apostle is not thinking of any of the nine or ninety-nine gifts from the Spirit: not all in the church are apostles, teachers, healers, or speakers in tongues (1 Cor. 12:28–30). Each is given at least one gift (12:7), and no one has every gift. But, praise God, every believer has the gift that is none other than the Spirit.

Paul assumes this about his readers in Rome also. Would you believe a "scandal" about God—that God declares the ungodly believer righteous (Rom. 4:5)? After illustrating his point with a trusting Abraham and a forgiven David, the apostle goes on in 5:1, "Therefore, since we are justified by faith, we have peace with God through our Lord Jesus Christ." Characterizing the believer's life as one of grace, of joy mixed with suffering, of endurance and hope, he concludes the paragraph, "God's love has been flooded into our hearts through the Holy Spirit who has been given to us" (Rom. 5:5, au. trans.). "To us," to Paul and all his Roman readers, was the Holy Spirit given. According to Paul, one does not belong to Christ without having his Spirit: "Any one who does not have the Spirit of Christ does not belong to him" (Rom. 8:9).

The glory of Christians, in all their shame, exultation, joy, and tribulation, is that their faith is a habitat for God's Spirit in Jesus.

Full of the Spirit

God fills with the Holy Spirit. One day some years ago, I read a letter announcing a conference on the Holy Spirit, which contained some interesting code words. Every speaker would be "Spirit-baptized," "Spirit-filled." As we have seen, the apostle Paul held that every one of those quarrelsome Corinthian believers had been Spirit-baptized, that is, baptized in the one Spirit into Christ's body. Because all of them had been caused to drink of the one Spirit, presumably all had been Spirit-filled. But what do "Spirit-baptized" and "Spirit-filled" mean in the code of that letter?

"Fullness of the Spirit" is another term that is often tossed about among Christians. How many times does that phrase appear in the New Testament? Not once! But "to be filled with the Spirit" and "to be full of the Spirit"—that is New Testament language. Let us go on now to several aspects of God's filling with the Spirit.

Sometimes being filled with the Spirit refers to God's initial filling or baptizing. We have noted that several times in the Gospels, John the Baptist predicts that Jesus is the one who will baptize with the Holy Spirit. The fulfillment began on Pentecost.

Creation, fall, exodus, incarnation, crucifixion, resurrection, ascension, Pentecost, Jesus' visible return—are these not major events in God's dealings with people, the planet, and the universe? Since by *proclaiming* these unique and unrepeatable acts, God is reclaiming all creation, the preaching and trusting in Christ are also major events. As far as Pentecost is concerned, we cannot overestimate its importance— since it is welded to the cross and resurrection!

Luke's account is well known. On Pentecost, while the disciples waited in Jerusalem for the Spirit, there was the sound like the rush of a mighty wind and the appearance of tongues as of fire. "And they were all filled with the Holy Spirit and began to speak in other tongues, as the Spirit gave them utterance" (Acts 2:4).

Pentecost fulfilled John the Baptist's prophecy about Jesus the Baptizer. In the account, Peter proclaims about Jesus, "Being therefore exalted at the right hand of God, and having received from the Father the promised Holy Spirit, he has poured out this which you see and hear" (Acts 2:33, au. trans.). Now that Jesus is glorified, the Spirit of God is in Jesus Christ the Lord (John 7:39); the Spirit is poured out and people are filled.

As we have seen, Luke reports that those filled "began to speak in other tongues, as the Spirit gave them utterance." This is speaking that can be immediately understood. Those filled with the Spirit speak in languages foreign to themselves but understood by the Pentecost pilgrims to Jerusalem as their own languages. These devout people are bewildered, yet they understand the speakers to be "telling in our own tongues the mighty works of God" (Acts 2:11).

The event is without parallel before or since Pentecost. Is this not precisely Luke's point? Pentecost, like the incarnation, is unrepeatable. A new age, the last, has fully dawned. Jesus is alive: Jesus is Lord, and his Spirit has been given to illuminate him for all humankind. It is noteworthy that the experience of speaking and hearing intelligible languages described in Acts 2 is different from the unintelligible speaking in tongues discussed by Paul in 1 Corinthians 12—14 which is forbidden unless an interpreter is present.

Pentecost itself is unique, just as Jesus had one birthday, one crucifixion. The consequences of the Spirit's coming, however, continue, as do the consequences of the incarnation and crucifixion. Joel's prophecy that God would pour out the Spirit on all flesh, and that sons and daughters, menservants and maidservants would prophesy, was being fulfilled on the spot by the apostles: Peter powerfully proclaimed the crucified and resurrected Jesus who pours forth God's Spirit. The Holy Spirit used Peter's sermon to bring some three thousand people to repent, to believe, to be baptized in Jesus Christ's name, to receive forgiveness and the gift that is the Spirit.

What Jesus does according to Acts 2 fulfills the predictions in the Gospels and Acts that he will "baptize in the Holy Spirit." Therefore, the verb "filled" in Acts 2:4 ("They were all filled with the Holy Spirit") is in this context the equivalent of "baptize." Not always, however, is "filled" used with this meaning, as we shall discover. There is one further instance in Acts where "filled with the Holy Spirit" has reference to God's initial filling.

Stopped by the living Christ on the Damascus road, Paul was blinded and had to be led to that city. There, under divine guidance, a disciple named Ananias befriended him. Anxious at first because of Paul's bad reputation, Ananias upon further guidance searched Paul out. "He said, 'Brother Saul, the Lord Jesus who appeared to you . . . has sent me that you may regain your sight and be filled with the Holy Spirit.' And immediately something like scales fell from his eyes and he regained his sight. Then he rose and was baptized, and took food and was strengthened" (Acts 9:17–19). This passage seems to say that Paul became a disciple of Christ after he had met Jesus, acknowledged him as Lord, and been baptized and filled with the Spirit. Beginning with the three thousand on Pentecost, being baptized and filled with the Holy Spirit are normally bound together in a being "born of water and the Spirit." Before Pentecost the apostles had already received "water baptism" from John the Baptist. As for "rebaptism," its denial can be succinctly expressed: "The simplest thing to say about rebaptism is that it is impossible."[3] But those who have been *baptized* with the Holy Spirit on Pentecost are later *filled* with the Holy Spirit, more than once!

Spirit fillings can take place after God's once-for-all baptizing in the Spirit. After Peter and John healed a cripple through Jesus' name (Acts 3:16), the authorities arrested them. Peter and John were brought the next day before the Jerusalem authorities and asked, "By what power or by what name did you do this?" (Acts 4:7). "Then Peter, filled with the Holy Spirit" names "the name of Jesus Christ of Nazareth." After their release, the two apostles rejoined their friends and reported what had occurred. The group raised a stout cry to God to "grant to thy servants to speak thy word with all boldness. . . . And when they had prayed, . . . they were all filled with the Holy Spirit and spoke the word of God with boldness" (4:29–31).

A parallel experience is recorded about Paul later in Acts. Paul was confronted in Cyprus by a magician, Elymas, who was trying to turn the Roman proconsul Sergius Paulus away from the faith. "Paul, filled with the Holy Spirit, looked intently at" this hinderer and caused him to be stricken blind for a time (Acts 13:4–11).

The common denominator in these three instances of the use of the phrase "filled with the Holy Spirit" is that each deals with an occasion when one Christian or a group in crisis was empowered for action by God's filling with the Spirit.

There are two other passages in the New Testament that speak of being filled with the Spirit, one in Acts, the other in Ephesians. Since joy is a "fruit of the Spirit," it is not surprising to find "joy" and other terms that are related to joy in contexts where God's filling with the Spirit is involved. The context of Acts 13:52 describes what Paul, Barnabas, and the new disciples in Iconium were experiencing after the apostles had been hounded out of Antioch by prominent women and men of the city. "And the disciples were being filled with joy and the Holy Spirit" (13:52, au. trans.). This being continuously filled is corroborated by a very interesting passage outside Acts. In Eph. 5:18 it is written, "And do not get drunk with wine, for that is debauchery; but be filled with the Spirit." Since these Christians in Ephesus are addressed as saints in Christ Jesus (1:1), they have already been baptized in the Spirit. The juxtaposition of the concepts "drunk with wine" and "filled with the Spirit" is eye-catching (see Acts 2:13). Is there something about being "intoxicated" with the Spirit of the crucified, risen Jesus that resembles being "high" with the spirits of Dionysus? In the passage from Ephesians, however, drunkenness is decisively contrasted with being "filled with the Spirit."

Let us note several significant aspects of this clause. First, "Be filled with the Spirit" is a command. Second, it is in the passive: the hearers are not urged to "fill your own selves" or to "fill each other" with the Spirit but rather are urged to "be filled with the Spirit." Third, the verb of command is plural: *all* members of the Ephesian church are urged to be filled with the Spirit. Fourth, the imperative verb is (in the Greek) in the present tense; it is not in the Greek tense that involves a command to once-for-all action. The verb form used here indicates *continuing* action: "Keep being filled with the Spirit" (au. trans.).

"Keep being filled with the Spirit." But how? How else but in the context of the fellowship of believers, with its horizontal and vertical aspects? Here the believers are "addressing one another in psalms and hymns and spiritual songs . . . always and for everything giving thanks in the name of our Lord Jesus Christ to God the Father" (Eph. 5:19–20). How richly the word of the Suffering Servant and Lord Christ dwells in Christians singing a hymn about the "one obedient even to death on a cross" (Phil. 2:6–11 is thought by many to be a very early Christian hymn adapted by Paul)! This kind of hymnody constitutes a "new song" (Rev. 5:9–10) the like of which could not even be imagined before the Lamb was slain to take away the sin of the world, thereby ushering in the end time.

As the Ephesians yielded themselves to God's constant filling with
his Spirit, they were being prepared to respond knowledgeably and
positively to the words that in the Greek text close the paragraph under
discussion: "Be subject to one another out of reverence for Christ."

Persons are full of the Holy Spirit. The phrase "full of the Holy
Spirit" is used to describe Jesus after his baptism (Luke 4:1). Victori-
ous over the tempter, Jesus returned to Galilee in the power of the
Spirit. In the Nazareth synagogue he claimed to be the one anointed for
mission by the Lord's Spirit.

In Acts there are two other occurrences of the term. Rather early at
"First Church" in Jerusalem, Greek-speaking Jews "murmured against
the Hebrews because their widows were neglected in the daily distribution" (Acts 6:1). The Twelve assembled the disciples and suggested that
they elect a board of seven to correct the matter, "seven men of good
repute, full of the Spirit and of wisdom." Having agreed, the congregation elected seven men. Among them was Stephen, a "man full of faith
and of the Holy Spirit." His opponents "could not withstand the
wisdom and the Spirit with which he spoke" and brought Stephen to
trial before the Jewish authorities. Answering charges of blasphemy, he
gave an oral survey of Israel's history from Abraham to Jesus, closing
with a stinging accusation that his stiff-necked hearers had betrayed and
murdered the Righteous One. With his audience aroused to teeth-
grinding fury, Stephen, "full of the Holy Spirit" (7:55), saw a vision
of the glory of God, with Jesus at God's right hand. Cast out of the city
to be stoned, Stephen prayed as the rocks flew, "Lord Jesus, receive my
spirit." Before dying he interceded, "Lord, do not hold this sin against
them" (7:60).

"Full of the Holy Spirit" is used to describe only one other person
in the New Testament: Barnabas. When Paul first came to Jerusalem
after his conversion, Barnabas introduced him to the apostles. The
persecution after Stephen's martyrdom scattered believers into Cyprus
and Syria, and they preached the Lord Jesus and made many converts.
Hearing of this, the Jerusalem church elected Barnabas their delegate
to Antioch. "When he came and saw the grace of God, he was glad;
and he exhorted them all to remain faithful to the Lord with steadfast
purpose; for he was a good man, full of the Holy Spirit and of faith"
(Acts 11:23-24). Presently Barnabas found Paul in Tarsus and brought
him to Antioch, where the disciples were first called Christians.

Full of the Holy Spirit! What does it mean? In the passages just cited, this phrase seems to point toward the condition or state of a person who listens to and heeds God's Spirit. It is not merely a sporadic state; rather, for such persons, trusting God and yielding to the persuasive Spirit constitute a constant way of life. This is the case with Jesus, and only with him is this perfectly true. "Full of the Holy Spirit," he conquered the tempter, taught, preached, healed, and exorcised "by the finger [Spirit] of God." Obedient trust, however, was not automatic for Jesus. He "learned obedience through what he suffered" (Heb. 5:8), from Bethlehem through Gethsemane to Calvary. Stephen, "full of faith and the Holy Spirit," vigorously proclaimed Christ, courageously and calmly met violent death, and compassionately interceded for his murderers. "Full of the Holy Spirit and of faith," Barnabas was generous in his gifts to the earliest church and dared to introduce the unpopular Paul, former persecutor of Christians, to the apostles. Characterized by the apostles as "son of encouragement," he seemingly had a gift of persuading people to take heart in the Lord Christ. Both Stephen and Barnabas are characterized as "full of faith" as well as "full of the Holy Spirit."

Full of the Holy Spirit! Does this ascription not mean to have the mind of Christ, to be full of the courageous and compassionate Spirit of Jesus, ready for anything, zestful for life, wherever the Spirit leads, even to death? What could be more significant work for the Holy Spirit of God than to keep filling with Christ's Spirit those who have been baptized into the Spirit, so that they may be "little Christs"?

4

The Spirit Gives
Manifold Gifts

There are three major passages in the New Testament concerning charisms, or gifts of grace. They are Rom. 12:3-8; 1 Corinthians 12—14; and Eph. 4:7-12. Since the exercise of spiritual gifts was causing problems in Corinth, Paul took great pains to counsel the Christians there. First Corinthians is therefore a good place to begin.

The Corinthians were a gifted but chaotic church. In this epistle Paul is employing his apostolic gifts to help his readers function effectively as members of their congregation. First, as he continues to answer a letter from Corinth (see 1 Cor. 7:1), he does not make clear whether he is writing about spiritual things or spiritual people (12:1); the word he uses could refer to either. Then Paul mentions the ecstatic religious experiences with dumb idols which the Corinthians had in their pre-Christian days. He proceeds to answer a twofold question they had apparently asked him about the inspiration behind two very different statements. Paul replies, "No one speaking by the Spirit of God ever says 'Jesus be cursed!' and no one can say 'Jesus is Lord' except by the Holy Spirit" (1 Cor. 12:3). Is it not almost unthinkable that a Christian congregation should ask whether "Jesus be cursed" is inspired by the Holy Spirit? It may be that there was a "Christ party" at Corinth (see 1:12) who were so carried away with the heavenly, spiritual Christ, as opposed to the earthly, fleshly Jesus, that they cried out, "Cursed be Jesus!" At any rate, the spirit who inspires such is not holy. The Holy Spirit does, however, evoke the fundamental Christian confession "Jesus is Lord." The content of inspired speech indicates its source, according to Paul.

A recurring emphasis in Paul that has generally not been sufficiently noticed in discussions about spiritual gifts begins in the next verses: "Varieties of charismata . . . varieties of services . . . varieties of workings" (12:4–6). With Paul's emphasis on *varieties* of gifts, can we assume that all will be included in the list in the next few verses? Some apparently think so.

For the Common Good

The significance of the next verse can scarcely be exaggerated: "To each is given the manifestation of the Spirit for the common good" (12:7). *Each* believer is given a gift; not one is giftless! The verb is a "divine passive": God is the donor. The last part of the verse is as important as the rest: each is given a manifestation of the Spirit *for the common good.* This last phrase is a key to everything Paul says about charisms. Therefore this red thread of Paul's thought will be followed.

The cruciality of using a spiritual gift for the common good is spotlighted in Paul's discussion of Christ's body. "For just as the body is one and has many members, and all the members of the body, though many, are one body, so it is with Christ. For in one Spirit we were all baptized into one body—Jews or Greeks, slaves or free—and all were caused to drink of one Spirit" (12:12–13, au. trans.). In the next paragraph the apostle states that in a body, every member is different; if such great diversity should cause a member to say, "I do not belong to the body because I am not some other member," it is still a part of the body. If the whole body were an eye, what a monstrosity! But more important, there would be no hearing or smelling, in fact, no body. No part can say to another, "I have no need for you." In fact, the seemingly weaker parts are indispensable.

The common good is stressed again by Paul as he becomes even more explicit about the body: "Now you are the body of Christ and individually members of it" (12:27). In Romans a still greater emphasis on members' mutuality occurs: "We, though many, are one body in Christ, and individually members one of another" (12:5). Members of Christ's body are even *members of one another*—that is intimacy!

The love chapter, 1 Corinthians 13, is positioned where it is to stress sharply that gifts without love are useless. Without love, gifts of tongues, prophecy, or knowledge, or even of the handing-over of one's body for burning, amount to nothing.

First Corinthians 14 intensifies the emphasis on mutuality. "Make love your aim, and earnestly desire the spiritual gifts, especially that you may prophesy." Prophecy edifies the church. If it is interpreted, speaking in tongues edifies believers. These verses are mentioned here simply because of their profound eloquence in underscoring that charisms are "for the common good," for building up all members of the congregation.

Of a piece is Paul's next question: "If I come to you speaking in tongues, how shall I benefit you unless I bring you some revelation or knowledge or prophecy or teaching?" Paul concludes the paragraph with another ringing plea "for the common good": "So with your-selves; since you are eager for manifestations of the Spirit, strive to excel in building up the church" (14:6-12).

In the remainder of the chapter the author continues his emphasis on congregational practices that result in edification. Prayer during wor-ship is to be so intelligible that even a novice will know when to say amen (vv. 13-19). Unintelligible tongues are useless for evangelism, but prophecy can convict and convert unbelievers (vv. 20-25).

Paul assumes that when the congregation assembles, each member will make a contribution toward building up the church. "Let all things be done for edification," he reiterates (v. 26). Later, in the final part of the chapter, the apostle lays down guidelines for orderly and edifying services of worship by and for members with various gifts of the Spirit. "For God is not a God of confusion but of peace" (v. 33). Paul makes the apostolic claim that "what I am writing to you is a command of the Lord" (v. 37) and exhorts that "all things should be done decently and in order" (v. 40).

How Manifold Are the Gifts?

In connection with Paul's emphasis in 1 Cor. 12:4-6 on the *varieties* of gifts, we asked whether gifts might be involved beyond the nine listed in 1 Cor. 12:7-11. This is a relevant question, because some actu-ally recognize only the nine. It is now time to answer that question.

In chapter 12, after describing the body the apostle writes, "And God has appointed in the church first apostles, second prophets, third teach-ers, then workers of miracles, then healers, helpers, administrators, speakers in various kinds of tongues" (12:28). Although it is not evident in most translations, Paul first mentions three kinds of gifted *people:*

apostles, prophets, teachers. He then adds some *gifts:* miracles, gifts of healing, helpful deeds, administrative gifts. But the main point here is that apostles and teachers are not specifically mentioned in 12:7-11, and helpful deeds and administrative gifts are totally new in 12:28. Romans 12:6-8 gives additional proof that the nine charisms listed first in 1 Corinthians 12 are not intended to be exhaustive. In Romans, eight of those original nine are missing, and added to prophecy, which is common to the two lists, are five gifts not mentioned in either: service, exhortation, contributions, helping, showing mercy. Ephesians 4:11 mentions two categories of gifted people not previously mentioned: evangelists and pastors. It is obvious that the charisms are more than merely nine. As we noted, people and gifts are listed together in 1 Cor. 12:28, three of one and five of the other. In Rom. 12:6-8 there is a new variation on the theme. Here the gifts come first and are followed by the gifted people—two of one, six of the other. What is to be made of all this?

Ephesians 4 may shed further light on the number of spiritual gifts. The chapter begins with a challenge that believers lead a life worthy of their calling. The unity of those called is then emphasized. There is one body, one Spirit, one hope, one Lord, one faith, one baptism, and one God and Father of us all. After this is a section on gifts:

> But grace was given to each of us according to the measure of Christ's gift. Therefore it is said, "When he ascended on high he led a host of captives, and he gave gifts to men." (vv. 7-8)

Later the text continues,

> And [Christ] gave some apostles, some prophets, some evangelists, some pastors and teachers. (v. 11, au. trans.)

According to these verses, Christ gave gifts and gifted people to his church. It can be seen that in New Testament passages where the charisms are listed, there is a happy commingling of gifts and gifted persons.

The reason the New Testament authors can so easily glide between the charism and the charismatic person is that these two are as inseparable as belief and the believer. There is no gift floating around apart from a baptized believer who uses it. Conversely, there is no Christian without a charism. "To *each* is given the manifestation of the

Spirit for the common good." But the charisms are not merely nine in number; they are ninety times nine. There are as many charisms as there are Christians.

Paul's extended section on the body celebrates this (1 Cor. 12:12–27). All were baptized in one Spirit into Christ's body, all were caused to drink of one Spirit. Every member belongs to the body with a function indispensable for the well-being of the body. Seeing requires an eye and hearing an ear; an ear normally hears and an eye sees. Part and function belong together. Hence, both 1 Corinthians 12 and Romans 12 teach contrary to the position that there are only nine gifts.

The wrong question has too often been asked: What are the gifts of God's Spirit? Why not ask instead, *Who* are those gifted by God's Spirit? The answer is, *All* baptized believers are charismatic, Spirit-gifted. Not all of the many members in the one body have the same function, but they all have *some* function. All members of Christ's body, just as they are, with all their potential and all their limitations, are gifts of God's Spirit. No member is inconsequential.

To get at the same point from another angle: Does Paul mean to exclude any Christian at Corinth when he gives his second list in 1 Cor. 12:28? "And God has appointed in the church first apostles, second prophets, third teachers, then workers of miracles, then healers, helpers, administrators, speakers in various kinds of tongues." A Stephanas might say to himself hearing this, "An apostle I am not, but a helper I try to be." This is no mere flight of fancy, because Stephanas and his household were probably Paul's first converts in Corinth (1 Cor. 16:15); Paul himself baptized them. And this Corinthian must have felt his charism confirmed when he heard a few remarks in the last part of Paul's letter: "You know that the household of Stephanas were the first converts in Achaia, and they have devoted themselves to the service of the saints" (1 Cor. 16:15). Stephanas and his household had been employing their Spirit-given charisms whether they realized it or not, devoting "themselves to the service of the saints." They had labored "for the common good" of the congregation, and that is what charism is all about.

Is there anything, then, that cannot be a charism? Any gift devoted to the service of the saints for the common good is a charism. The notion of charism is as inclusive as that of justification. Forgiveness is for each one who believes in the God who declares the ungodly righteous. By this each believer becomes a saint (a sinner forgiven), as Christ's welcoming notorious sinners to table fellowship so potently proclaims. No one who enters is cast out. God has poured out the Spirit on all humankind in these last days since Pentecost. Each believer is Spirit-baptized and "to each is given the manifestation of the Spirit for the common good."

It is not the case, however, that a charism is necessarily a permanent possession of a believer. The Spirit of Christ is a permanent resident. A charism, however, is more like a transitory guest. Apostleship in the narrow sense may be one exception. By the strictest definition an apostle is one who was with Jesus from the days of John the Baptist till his ascension. Of these there were only several more than a baker's dozen. Paul claimed apostleship because he had seen the risen Lord and been commissioned by him. Even his claim did not go unchallenged, however. At any rate, apostles were unique because Jesus was crucified and resurrected only once. This does not mean that an apostle was infallible. An apostle could be dead wrong, as Peter was at Antioch when Paul withstood him "eyeball to eyeball" (Gal. 2:11–14). Nevertheless, Peter was still an apostle. There were, on the other hand, false apostles. And there was Judas, whom the Father had given to Jesus, who turned aside from the ministry and apostleship. Apart from apostleship, the charisms do not seem permanent possessions. There are different kinds of charisms. Not all in the congregation can lay claim to each kind. In principle each believer may from time to time enjoy any charism. Since this was true of prophecy—"You can all prophesy one by one"—the same seems likely of other charisms as well.

How manifold are the gifts and the gifted? How many and how varied are they? They are at least as manifold as the baptized believers in Christ's body, the church. No member of that lively body is without a vital function. The Spirit has made some parts magnificently versatile. Succeeding chapters will suggest some of the implications of these facts.

5

All Christians Are Given Charisms

I first observed that the term "charismatic" today generally has three meanings. In the secular sphere it describes people who can stir popular support and enthusiasm. Second, it is used by some Christians to describe the gifts listed in 1 Corinthians, Romans, and Ephesians (especially healing, prophecy, and speaking in and interpreting tongues) as well as to describe those who employ these gifts. On this usage, only certain Christians are designated charismatics. Third, the word is employed in a broader sense by Christians who are convinced that the New Testament teaches that all Christians are baptized in the Spirit. On this usage, since "each is gifted . . . for the common good," all Christians are charismatic.

The attribution of charismatic gifts to all Christians is fairly common. The English theologian and exegete Michael Green writes,

> There is no division between charismatics and noncharismatics, between "haves" and "have-nots" in the one-class community of Christ. All alike are charismatics; for all alike are eternally in debt in the sheer charis of God who . . . equipped us with varying gifts.[4]

The Roman Catholic scholar Hans Küng holds the same position. In the context of a reference to the gifts of grace cited in Rom. 12:6–8, he writes that "charisms are not limited to a particular set of persons but are given to each and every Christian."[5] Ernst Käsemann echoes the position:

> "As Christians themselves . . . are members of the body of Christ, are they all, in so far as they are true to their condition, endowed with charisma?" To put the question is to answer "yes" to it.[6]

The New Testament evidence marshaled in the preceding chapters allows us to decide which employment of "charismatic" is the more appropriate in a Christian context: to designate mainly those who heal, prophesy, speak in tongues, and interpret them, or rather to describe all Christians with their entire range of gifts from God's prodigal Spirit. Christians today and others, including the readers of this book, are challenged to answer this question "for the common good."

In the present chapter, "charismatic" will be used with a comprehensive reference. What is life like among charismatic Christians, each with a gift from the Spirit? The answers that I shall develop will be rooted in the New Testament lists of the charisms and the gifted but will not neglect other important aspects of the charismatic either.

Here is a brief, working definition of gifts of grace: Charisms are gifts from God's Spirit to all of God's children in Christ; to each is given a gift for the common good, whether the gift is newly bestowed or it is a fresh activation of a latent potentiality.

There are various ways in which the charisms may be grouped. In this book they will be considered under the two broad headings that some authors of the New Testament came to imply. Consider the exhortation in 1 Peter: "As each has received a gift [*charisma*], employ it for one another as good stewards of God's varied grace: whoever speaks, as one who utters oracles of God; whoever renders service, as one who renders it by the strength which God supplies" (4:10–11). The two general categories are, then, "gifts of speaking" and "gifts of serving." Obviously, the two are not mutually exclusive.

Gifts of Speaking

Apostles. The Christian church was born the moment that some people were convinced by God's Spirit that Jesus is Lord. Matthew, Mark, and Luke tell of God's revelation to the Twelve that Jesus is Messiah and of Peter's confession of that truth. But believing that Jesus is the Christ is not the same as believing that Jesus (Christ) is Lord. There are some aspects of this later confession that need to be stressed. First, it belongs to the time after the crucifixion and resurrection of Jesus. Second, it is a credo that arises in connection with the resurrection appearances but not merely because of them. "Jesus is alive" is a presupposition of "Jesus is Lord" but not its equivalent, since others have been raised from the dead. Third, like the confession that Jesus is Messiah, the confession that Jesus is Lord is wrought by God, not by mere humans. There is a certain parallelism between Matt. 16:17 and 1 Cor. 12:3b. In the former, Jesus says to Peter after his confession, "You are the Christ": "Blessed are you, Simon Bar-Jona! For flesh and blood has not revealed this to you, but my Father who is in heaven." Paul writes in the latter, "No one can say 'Jesus is Lord' except by the Holy Spirit."

From the evidence it looks as if the risen Jesus appearing in the Spirit convinced the disciples that he is Lord and got them moving as his apostles, those commissioned to be his ambassadors.

According to the Fourth Gospel, Jesus appeared to the disciples on Easter evening in Jerusalem, behind doors locked for fear of the Jews. The disciples recognized the Lord, who commissioned them. A week later Jesus appeared to Thomas, who had been absent Easter evening. After their encounter, Thomas's ringing confession erupts: "My Lord and my God!" (John 20:19–28).

The Book of Acts teaches that there was a new dimension to the disciples' faith when Jesus Messiah returned as Lord in God's Spirit. The climax of Peter's powerful Pentecost proclamation is "Let all the house of Israel therefore know assuredly that God has made him both Lord and Christ, this Jesus whom you crucified" (Acts 2:36). According to a later section of Acts, something decisive happened to the disciples' faith on Pentecost (see Acts 11:16–17). Peter here says that Pentecost was for him and his hearers a time "when we believed in the Lord Jesus Christ." Remarkable! Their faith had a necessary *new* dimension because of the new revelation that Jesus is Lord!

Indispensable, then, to the resurrection faith of the earliest church is the Lord's Spirit, convincing people that the living Jesus is Lord. As Paul teaches, "God's love has overflowed our hearts through the Holy Spirit who has been given to us" (Rom. 5:5, au. trans.).

Very early in Acts reference is made to the apostles whom Jesus had chosen. In two of the three Pauline lists of gifts, the apostles are mentioned first (1 Cor. 12:28; Eph. 4:11), both because of their chronological priority and because they had been commissioned to be *the* witnesses par excellence to the death and resurrection of Jesus and the *meaning* of these events: "Jesus Christ is Lord." A mere twenty-five years after all this, Paul wrote the Corinthians to remind them of the saving Gospel they had heard from him: "For I delivered to you as of first importance what I also received, that Christ died for our sins in accordance with the scriptures, and that he appeared to Cephas, then to the twelve" (1 Cor. 15:3–5).

The apostles were those who had both seen the risen Lord and been commissioned by the risen One himself to preach the Gospel. In the salutation of most of the epistles, Paul identifies himself as an apostle, and in Acts 14:14 he and Barnabas are called apostles. Besides these two, the Twelve, James the Lord's brother, and Junias and Andronicus (Rom. 16:7), no other apostles in the strict sense of the term are known. In the annals of church history there are others called apostles, but they are so only in a secondary sense. Left to us, however, is the apostolic testimony, the means and norm for the church's faith and life.

From the risen Jesus on the Damascus road, Paul received his gospel, handed on and confirmed through fellow apostles and disciples. This gospel he and the other apostles and disciples proclaimed both to those who had never heard and to believers, including those who received the gifts to continue evangelizing. Insofar as apostles and the evangelists succeeding them proclaimed the Gospel to *create* the life of faith, hope, and love, they shared a common charism, obviously indispensable for the very existence as well as the continuing growth of the church.

Prophets. Occurring just after "apostles" in 1 Cor. 12:28 and Eph. 4:11 is "prophets"; in the list in Romans, apostles are not mentioned and "prophecy" is first.

Here is a brief but inclusive definition of prophecy in the earliest church:

> Primitive Christian prophecy is the inspired speech of charismatic preachers through whom God's plan of salvation for the world and the community and His will for the life of individual Christians are made known.[7]

Inspired by God's Spirit, the prophet may be a foreteller or a "forth-teller" or both. Agabus foretold a world famine (Acts 11:28) and predicted Paul's being seized at Jerusalem (Acts 21:10–14). More important, the Christian prophet speaks forth what God has done, is doing, and will have people do, in the world. This is perhaps clearest in Paul, who as an apostle functioned prophetically with his churches, bringing them revelation, knowledge, prophecy, and teaching. One who speaks in tongues speaks to God and is thereby edified, whereas one who prophesies speaks to people "for their upbuilding and encouragement and consolation" and the whole church is edified. Because prophecy contributes most "for the common good," Paul evaluates it as the most desirable and significant charism when he exhorts, "Make love your aim, and earnestly desire the spiritual gifts, especially that you may prophesy" (1 Cor. 14:1-6).

Paul's epistles illustrate clearly the content of Christian prophecy. As though present and speaking, he wrote to believers. He built them up by reminding them of the "mercies of God," exhorting and consoling on the same basis. His predictions dealt not merely with himself, but with the destiny of Jews, Christians, the race.

Prophecy is given through a revelation from God. The recipient, however, is not compelled to speak out immediately or interminably; God's Spirit both inspires and controls. Paul advises that in any given service at Corinth no more than two or three persons should prophesy, always one at a time. If one begins to prophesy and "if a revelation is made to another sitting by, let the first be silent," counsels Paul. "For you can all prophesy one by one, so that all may learn and all be encouraged; and the spirits of prophets are subject to prophets. For God is not a God of confusion but of peace" (1 Cor. 14:29-33).

Evidently women as well as men prayed and prophesied in early Christian services of worship (1 Cor. 11:4-5). Philip the evangelist "had four unmarried daughters who prophesied" (Acts 21:9). (In his infancy narratives, Luke mentions [chaps. 1—2] several inspired to prophesy: Elizabeth, Mary, Zechariah, Simeon, and the prophetess Anna.)

An aspect of primitive and early Christian prophecy which is sometimes overlooked calls for elaboration. In agreement with our definition of prophecy as the "inspired speech of charismatic preachers," we can say that Agabus prophesied about Paul's imminent fate in Jerusalem: "Thus says the Holy Spirit, 'So shall the Jews at Jerusalem bind the man who owns this girdle and deliver him into the hands of the Gentiles' " (Acts 21:10-11). Agabus claimed to be inspired—to speak for the Holy Spirit. Neither Paul nor anyone else contradicted his claim or his prophecy.

Further, some early Christian prophets break into exalted speech as though Christ is speaking through them in the first person. In the early part of the second century, Ignatius of Antioch claimed to speak with the "voice of God." *A Homily on the Preacher,* by Melito, bishop of Sardis, later in the same century, contains this element. At the close of his *Homily,* Melito ceases preaching *about* the Lord and begins to prophesy with a change that startles: "Who will contend against me? Let him stand before me. . . . I am the Lamb slain for you. . . . I am your resurrection. . . ." The style of Melito still shines through, but there is a general heightening as he is moved to speak forth as representing Jesus.[8] But in the latter part of the same century, prophecy came into rather general disrepute because of Montanus and two prophetesses, Prisca and Maximilla: these women prophesied that the heavenly Jerusalem would descend to two towns in Phrygia, where all Christians were to gather.[9]

When this prophecy and others proved false, true prophecy began to wane in the church; happily, by the close of the first century, Paul's epistles began to be read as Scripture, and toward the second half of the second century, the four Gospels attained the same high status in the church. Because the authoritative apostolic testimony to the Gospel was readily available during the worship of the congregation, through reading, proclamation, the sacraments, hymns, creeds, and other sharing, the general lack of prophecy in the primitive sense was not so serious as it might have been. When it seemed fairly evident to some that Christ's visible return might not occur immediately and that the church would be around awhile, officials in the church took over some of the functions that prophets had performed.

Is there prophecy today? Since apostles in the strict sense (those who had seen the risen Jesus and had been commissioned by him) functioned only in the earliest church, some now think that prophecy as known in the first centuries was also meant to be restricted to early times. But others, especially some participants in recent and current neo-Pentecostal movements, claim that the gift of prophecy is being received and exercised among and by them today. Since there is evidence of this gift among Christians beyond apostolic times, is there anything ruling it out in principle in our days?

Evangelists, pastors, and teachers. First Corinthians and Romans were written in the fifties of the first century, whereas Ephesians was composed decades later and reflects the outlook of the church then. The author considers the apostles and prophets to constitute a band with unparalleled significance in the church; the "household of God" is "built upon the foundation of the apostles and prophets, Christ Jesus himself being the chief cornerstone" (2:19–20). Having received the original revelation, through which God keeps creating the church, they possess a continuing and unique importance for having handed it on. In 1 Cor. 12:28, Paul almost certainly thinks of apostles as having this indispensable role in the church universal, but as he goes on with prophets, teachers, and others of the gifted, he is more likely thinking of that church as manifest in the Corinthian believers. If, then, the author of Ephesians includes apostles and prophets in one category, he may think of prophets as itinerant proclaimers of the gospel but not as having the authority bestowed on the apostles, the ambassadors plenipotentiary of the resurrected Jesus.

The "evangelists, pastors, and teachers" are those carrying on their ministries in the congregations of their day. Evangelists are the originally itinerant successors of the apostles and prophets, heralding God's good news in Christ primarily to the unconverted. All the apostles are evangelists, but not all evangelists are apostles, because the apostles have been directly commissioned by the risen Lord. Philip, the only person in the New Testament to be called an evangelist, was originally one of the Jerusalem church seven appointed to serve tables while the apostles devoted themselves to prayer and to the ministry of the Word. From the earliest church, then, there were people evangelizing. After the stoning of Stephen, the Jerusalem church was persecuted, and we read, "Now those who were scattered went about preaching the word. Philip went down to a city of Samaria, and proclaimed to them the Christ." Later in Acts 8, Philip is shown meeting the Ethiopian, to whom "he told . . . the good news of Jesus." At the end of the chapter he is described as preaching the gospel to all the towns from Azotus to Caesarea, where he had a house (Acts 21:8). It is at this point in Acts that he who had long been evangelizing on various roads and in scattered cities is called an evangelist. What originally was a function became in some instances more and more associated with a person or persons who were thought of as holding an office. Timothy is exhorted to "do the work of an evangelist" (2 Tim. 4:5), and he served with Paul in the gospel. Since unbelievers must hear the gospel to come alive, and believers to stay alive in Christ, an evangelist might function as a missionary or as a resident leader of a congregation. Although Paul was often on the move, he stayed some years evangelizing Ephesus. The evangelist's gift and function consist in proclaiming God's good news in Jesus Christ.

Are there evangelists in the church today? Certainly! Every teller of the evangel, the good news, is an evangelist; every true Christian preacher is one. There are contemporary preachers throughout the world who are generally acknowledged to have the gift of an evangelist. Technique is not the criterion here but content, the story of the crucified, risen Jesus. Do some have more of a gift than others? Do they have a more burning vision of those lost without Christ? Do they work harder, agonize more over getting out of the gospel's way, to set it straight and shout it out?

There are lay preaching evangelists. Enoch Scotvold was a lay preaching evangelist called by the Evangelical Lutheran church. And there are lay nonpreaching evangelists.

"I don't think of myself as an evangelist," she says.

"Not me, either," adds her husband.

But all the evidence is to the contrary. Water of Life Lutheran Church exists in Newcastle, Maine, largely because Ralph and Gerry Poriss live there.

When they lived in Arizona, they enjoyed summer vacations in Maine, where they also collected art and antiques. On one of their trips, they bought a nice little house by a waterfall. Though the building had been a "bloody disaster," in a few years they had transformed it into a stunning house and an antique shop, Alewives Antiques. But there was no Lutheran church nearby. After church shopping at a new place every Sunday for two years, they came to Prince of Peace in Augusta. Finding the people "very gracious and warm," they kept going back and in the end joined the church.

But eventually they found the sixty-mile round trip tiring, especially over winter roads. Although they loved their church, they requested that it consider a "satellite mission." After a number of meetings, the congregation arranged for a service every Sunday evening at Booth Bay Harbor. Ralph and Gerry had "guaranteed" but eight people for the opening service; forty showed. Even before that evening, Ralph had confidently ordered hymnals inscribed "Water of Life Lutheran Church."

Largely because of Ralph and Gerry's evangelical ingenuity—backed by the unwavering commitment of Prince of Peace and its pastor and lay assistant, and supported by the synod at a critical point—Water of Life Lutheran Church now has a resident pastor serving them with two-thirds of his time.

What happened? "We were sent here," Gerry responds. They and others in Augusta and New Castle employed their gifts to establish a new base for evangelical outreach in New England.[10]

By the time Ephesians was written, the trend from function to office was taking place also with those who performed their ministries mostly in one congregation. Because of the original Greek construction for "pastors and teachers," it is more than likely that pastors and teachers constitute one and the same group of leaders, who are referred to by their several responsibilities.

Ephesians 4:11 is the only place in the New Testament that the word "pastor," or "shepherd," is used of a church leader. The infrequent use of the word may be tied to the bad reputation shepherds had in the first century because they were thought to be servants who stole the use of pasture lands and often the produce of the herd. At any rate, the word "shepherd" or "pastor" is used only this once for a congregational leader, but the related verb "to herd, tend, pasture" occurs several times (e.g., 1 Peter 5:2; Acts 20:28; John 21:16). From these contexts it can be deduced that the pastor is one exhorted to tend his flock as a free son, not as a greedy hireling, and not to be domineering but to lead by example. Feeding is a primary function of a good shepherd. He is to be alert for danger from without and people speaking perversely from within. The New Testament picture of the pastor is enhanced by the selfless Chief Shepherd (1 Peter 5:5), who unlike thieving and deserting hirelings lays down his life for the sheep.

To the church today its Lord gives pastors. The best are those knowing and zealously concerned for every sheep and lamb in their care, watching for and warning of wolves, appropriately leading, feeding while laying down their lives for their flocks. How blessed, how thankful, are those with pastors who effectively feed and lead, who strongly and tenderly tend them! Ezekiel warns that God is against the shepherds who feed themselves only.

In the gentile churches, by the middle of the first century there were evidently those spending much time and energy on teaching, for Paul writes, "Let him who is taught the word share all good things with him who teaches" (Gal. 6:6). "In the church at Antioch there were prophets and teachers," two of whom were Saul (Paul) and Barnabas (Acts 13:1). Probably all five who are named both prophesied and taught; surely

Barnabas and Paul did. Both prophecy and teaching are listed among the gifts of the Spirit in Rom. 12:6–7; in 1 Cor. 12:28 prophets and teachers are cited second and third after the apostles as those "God has appointed in the church."

There was a distinction between the function of pastors and that of teachers. In the period when Ephesians was written, the ministry of pastors was concerned especially with the leadership, feeding, and self-less defense of the flock against dangers from without and within. The ministry of teachers had more to do with the clear, ordered instruction of the sheep and lambs. There was, of course, overlap, and the same person was likely to do both shepherding and teaching. It is the teaching function that will now be examined more closely.

Though there is not usually a sharp distinction between teaching and the other ministries in the New Testament, there is a development toward distinguishing between them. "Jesus came into Galilee, preach-ing the gospel of God, and saying, 'The time is fulfilled, and the king-dom of God is at hand; repent, and believe in the gospel' " (Mark 1:14–15). Jesus came preaching God's reign. He came also teaching what that reign is like, often in parables. But there is surely no absolute distinction between the content of Jesus' preaching and that of his teaching. Jesus taught the so-called Sermon on the Mount. Ultimately Jesus alone is the kingly rule of God dawning among humankind, and it was Jesus who confronted people through his parables. Granted that he first announced the kingdom and then elucidated, the content of both his preaching and his teaching was the gospel of what God was doing through him. And there is a sense in which Jesus himself mingled with people as a kind of personified parable, a walking and talking absolution. The despised and underprivileged in Israel were especially swift to detect that "this man welcomes sinners and eats with them."

But as time went on, teaching tended to involve the presentation of the implications of the gospel. This began in Paul's epistles of the sixth decade A.D. (Galatians, Romans, Corinthians). Ephesians followed this trend, as did Acts. The last paragraph in Acts states that for two years in Rome, Paul was "preaching the kingdom of God and teaching about the Lord Jesus Christ quite openly and unhindered." By the time of the Pastoral Epistles there seems to be even more of a differentiation between preaching and teaching.

A father and mother appeared on a TV show with their three growing daughters, each girl a genius. "Did you do anything that might have contributed to this?" the parents were asked.

"The last several months of each pregnancy," the mother replied, "I spoke directly to the baby I was carrying, read aloud good literature, including poetry, played fine music, and tried to remain as calm as possible. Then when my baby was born, I continued all this."

"What kind of universe is this?" is the infant's unconscious question, from birth if not before. Responsive, friendly, caring, reliable, or uncommunicative, hostile, unconcerned, undependable? Stamped deeply within, the answers provided to this question profoundly affect the child for life. Could we say that those with children are by that very fact called to teach? In the congregation, in the church, others also are called.

What shall they teach? We ought to ask rather, *Whom* shall they teach? The answer is, God. To help with the answer these last centuries, God raised up a giant in the church, Doctor (i.e., Teacher) Martin Luther, who wrote the Small Catechism "in the plain form to be taught to the family by the head of the household." To baptized believers, *God* is to be taught, the One who has given us the Ten Commandments and whom we confess as Father Creator, Son Redeemer, and Holy Spirit Sanctifier. God is the One who has given us the Lord's Prayer, the Sacrament of Baptism, and the Sacrament of the Altar. Jesus' disciples are "to be taught to observe all he has commanded."

For instruction at various levels it is ultimately God who singles out teachers. God bestows the aptitudes, desires, and opportunities for learning in general, and for learning to teach in particular. God provides perceptive instructors, students, administrators, pastors, and laity to help select and place those recognized as being given the gift of teaching.

Ministers are to equip the saints to minister. Before I discuss the other charisms listed in Romans 12 and 1 Corinthians 12, the first part of Ephesians 4 needs to be examined more closely. Written considerably later than Romans and 1 Corinthians, Ephesians reflects the development of church offices. Nevertheless, the significance of the function of each member is also enhanced in this epistle.

After exhorting the Ephesians to lead a life worthy of their calling and to maintain their many-faceted, Spirit-given unity, the author writes about charisms given to individuals. "To each one of us grace was given according to the measure of Christ's gift" (v. 7). Since v. 8 is attached by a "therefore" to what precedes, gifts that are numerous seem to be in the picture: "Therefore it is said, 'When he ascended on high he led a host of captives, and he gave gifts to men.' " But the especially significant aspect of Ephesians 4 becomes clear when vv. 11 and 12 are taken together: "And he gave some apostles, some prophets, some evangelists, some pastors and teachers to equip the saints for the work of ministry for building up the body of Christ" (au. trans.). The ultimate goal of Christ's gifts is to build up his body. Christ gives pastors and teachers and the rest in order to equip his *people* for the work of *ministry.* In other words, the primary ministry of ministers is to equip church members to minister! There is no room here for a hierarchy hoarding all the ministering. Rather, every member of Christ's body is ipso facto a minister for building up the body. Tremendous are the gift and responsibility of being a pastor: to equip God's people for ministry! Just as tremendous are the gift and responsibility of being a member who is not a pastor: to be equipped for ministry and to do it! All Christians are charismatic. Where every member of a body is functioning as its Creator intended, there is a healthy body. It is evident that although Ephesians 4 seems to reflect a more developed church structure than 1 Corinthians 12 and Romans 12 do, it actually emphasizes the same view of the church as the body in which "grace was given to each of us according to the measure of Christ's gift." Ever since Adam and Eve, and Abraham and Sarah, God has been calling a *people,* not merely an elite within a people.

The overwhelming emphasis, then, in 1 Corinthians 12, Romans 12, and Ephesians 4 is that *all Christians are charismatic; every member is a minister.* Among all the ministers, there are some whose primary ministry is to equip the other members for ministry to build up Christ's body. Since all are members of the body, the mutuality of ministries is impressive. Because members are individually members of one another, when they minister to one another all are built up in the giving and in the receiving, and the body itself is built up.

There are several aspects of "building up the body of Christ" mentioned in this context in Ephesians. One is unity. There is a unity that is *given* (4:4–6), a unity *to be maintained* (v. 3), and a unity *to be attained* (vv. 11–13). Unity is an objective always to be striven for in the light of our fundamental unity in Christ's body.

"Building up the body of Christ" is a movement toward maturity, "to the measure of the stature of the fullness of Christ." Maturity is marked by stability of doctrine that is not tossed to and fro by crafty tricksters; it is marked too by honesty tempered with the sensitivity of love (vv. 12–16). The building-up of Christ's people is repeatedly emphasized as *the* criterion for the validity of any church practice (1 Cor. 14:4, 5, 12, 17, 26).

Fundamental in the building-up of Christ's body is *love.* "Rooted and grounded in love" and knowing the "love of Christ" (Eph. 3:17, 19), "who is the head" (4:15), each part will be nourished by him as it "upbuilds itself in love" (4:16). The mutuality of ministry receives as heavy an emphasis in 4:15–16 as in 4:11–12; the two sections shed light on each other.

Exhortation. Exhortation is designated a charism in Rom. 12:8 and actually practiced by Paul in Rom. 12:1–2, which begins, "I exhort you, therefore, sisters and brothers . . . " (au. trans.). When Paul wrote to the Corinthians, he was writing to a congregation he had himself founded. At the time he wrote to the Christians at Rome, he had never even visited them. Paul was, however, an apostle for all people, including the Romans. Tactfully he mentions the mutual encouragement in the faith that his impending visit will bring. Paul writes while poised to deliver a gift from the gentile churches to Jerusalem, a fact reflected by his expression of deep concern with the salvation of all humankind, Jew and gentile (see esp. chaps. 9—11). This is what lies behind his eloquent appeal for the Romans' intercessory prayers for his "service for Jerusalem" (15:30–32). Further, he hopes to evangelize Spain with the Roman Christians' help. In the light of his aims, it is significant that Paul discusses charisms in Romans. Moreover, in this letter he gives a considerably different list from those in 1 Corinthians and in Ephesians. The overarching theme in Romans is the righteousness in which God declares the ungodly sinner who believes in Jesus Christ to be forgiven, empowered by God's Spirit.

Chapter 12 begins, "I appeal to you therefore, brethren, by the mercies of God, to present your bodies as a living sacrifice." Through the mercies of God spelled out in chapters 1—11, Paul appeals to the Roman

Christians to dedicate their very selves, bodies and all, to God as a sacrifice that stays alive! "Do not be conformed to this world but be transformed." In making this appeal, Paul is himself employing a gift of the Spirit. And it is to *Christians* that he appeals to present their bodies to Christ! Is Paul advocating renewal, revival, among Christians? Is this related to what happened to some Macedonian Christians whose extreme poverty overflowed in a wealth of liberality? "First they gave themselves to the Lord" (2 Cor. 8:5).

When Paul continues, "For by the grace given to me . . . ," he is speaking as an apostle commissioned by the risen Lord. Claiming the authority of an apostle, he writes, "I bid every one among you not to think of himself more highly than he ought to think, but to think with sober judgment, each according to the measure of faith which God has assigned him." The word "faith" in this context seems to be used in the sense of the trust in Christ that all believers exercise; since all have it, faith is a solid basis for humble self-evaluation in relation to other believers. Verses 4–5 are about the body, its members, and their functions.

In vv. 6–8, Paul lists seven charisms. Of these only prophecy appears in the list of nine charisms in 1 Cor. 12:8–10. This fact corroborates the view that the various New Testament lists are suggestive, not exhaustive. And the contents of these three verses further demonstrate that the gifts are numerous and varied.

In presenting the next three gifts, Paul uses a phrase with each: "in our serving; . . . in his teaching; . . . in his exhortation." Perhaps there is a touch of "Cobbler, keep to your last" in what he says: Use your own gift; do not covet or attempt to use that of someone else.

With "he who teaches" (v. 7b) begins the listing of the last five gifts in this series; note that all five are persons. As in the other New Testament lists, there is a happy commingling of gifts and gifted persons.

Paraklesis. We are reminded once more that there is nothing automatic about exercising a charism. This reminder is built into the words of v. 8a: "he who exhorts, in his exhortation." The Greek verb here is exactly the same as the very first word of Romans 12, translated as "I appeal." The endowment denoted is highly significant; it is an aspect of Paul's apostolic prophetic gift, of which these first verses of Romans 12 are evidence. Yet this gift is for others besides the apostle. Its tremendous importance lies in its close relationship with the gospel of

Christ. On the one hand, paraklesis is a million miles distant from such harsh law as "Do this or be damned." On the other hand, it is not a mere moral appeal with no power behind it or in it. Paraklesis is always "through the mercies of God," "through the gentleness and meekness of Christ," or in a similar gospel context explicit or implied. Without the gospel there would be no paraklesis in this technical sense; it is rooted in the gospel and grows right out of it. The law has no power to give life, but the gospel of Jesus both makes alive and empowers life in the Spirit.

The function of paraklesis could well be designated the second use of the gospel. The gospel's primary function is to evoke faith in Jesus Christ; its second is to constitute the basis and the power for an obedient, responsive life in his Spirit.

A young man once stated that there had been only one person in his life who could exhort him effectively; perhaps that person had the gift of "paraklesis."

A woman facing tough times was urged by her pastor to hold on, to keep on keeping on; somehow this encouraged and helped her do so. Afterward she thanked the pastor for his encouragement, rooted in the gospel.

There is another very important meaning of the word "paraklesis." At many places in Paul's writings and elsewhere in the New Testament, "paraklesis" signifies "consoling help," "comfort," or "encouragement." Thus, the Old Testament was given not only for instruction but that through its *consolation* we might have hope (Rom. 15:4). Paul's inner striving for churches that he did not know personally was for their *encouragement* (Col. 2:2). As with exhortation, it is the mercy of God that is behind all this. God is praised as the "Father of mercies and God of all comfort, who comforts us in all our affliction, so that we may be able to comfort those who are in any affliction, with the comfort with which we ourselves are comforted by God" (2 Cor. 1:3–4). This meaning of "paraklesis" may be "traced back to the saving work of the triune God which leads those in need of help as supplicants to the Son of God, which is preached as exhortation in the power of the Spirit of God, and which carries with it already in this time the eternal comfort of God the Father."[11]

While paraklesis is part of the prophetic, apostolic ministry, it is also a part of the ministering of any member of the congregation who has received this gift. Because Paul saw encouraging and consoling as aspects of prophecy, he wrote, "Make love your aim, and earnestly desire the spiritual gifts, especially that you may prophesy. . . . For . . . he who prophesies speaks to men for their upbuilding and encouragement and consolation" (1 Cor. 14:1-3). "Let the one who has the gift of exhorting, use it." People thirst for encouragement.

A certain college president had this gift. In the middle of the night, as a campus building was burning to the ground, he was already dictating a letter to the pastors of the districts: "We will rebuild!" And they did! Exhorting the poorest parishioner or the wealthiest lumber baron, this college official got results. He had the gift of exhorting!

Two men drove far to be with their colleague at the funeral of his mother—to be there when not expected.

What a privilege it was for parents to be there for their wandering teenager, whose footsteps were heard pounding up the sidewalk in the dead of night, home at last.

God gives all these gifts and more. They are ours to use.

The utterance of wisdom and the utterance of knowledge. The congregation at Corinth was founded on Paul's second missionary campaign, around A.D. 50. Although by implication the apostle considered it a congregation confused, he addressed it as the "church of God," "sanctified in Christ Jesus, called to be saints" and "not lacking in any spiritual gift." But it was a factious church, its members saying, "I belong to Paul," or, "I belong to Apollos," or, "I belong to Cephas," or, "I belong to Christ" (1 Cor. 1:2-12).

Evidently the members of this church were enamored of a kind of wisdom and knowledge that did not grant due centrality to Christ crucified and to being known *by* God. Although they prided themselves on their spirituality, Paul could not address them as spiritual, since they were jealous and factious—still of the flesh. Their tendencies to despise the body were linked with a defense of incest and prostitution on the one hand, and with asceticism and marriage problems on the other.

What is Christian freedom in this context? Paul holds that the greatest freedom is that which one relinquishes out of caring for the welfare of a sister or brother. The apostle goes on to warn that it is possible to fall out of right relationship with God even though God is faithful. Paul commends the congregation for some worship practices, but he strenuously objects to others. He charges that the members' factiousness has made a shambles of the love feast and the Lord's Supper: "For in eating, each one goes ahead with his own meal, and one is hungry and another is drunk" (11:21). Finally, some of the Corinthians are saying "that there is no resurrection of the dead" (15:12). Apparently, in their enthusiasm for their present experiences, some have lost sight of the hope Christians have of the return of their risen Lord to consummate God's reign.

In the early chapters of this epistle, Paul is answering questions put to him by the Corinthians. As he begins the section dealing with "spiritual gifts" (12:1), he reminds his readers of their ecstatic experiences during their pre-Christian days. The fundamental speaking by the Holy Spirit's inspiration is the core christological confession "Jesus is Lord." Without this, all other ecstatic speech is meaningless. Only once this has been forcefully stated can other gifts be discussed.

First Paul emphasizes that all the gifts, including service and working, have their source in the triune God. Paul has shifted to the word *charismata* here (from *pneumatika*, v. 1), likely to stress that it is by grace (*charis*) that spiritual persons are what they are. By bringing in the word "service" (v. 5), the apostle gives notice that in Christ's church, day-to-day helping acts are on a par with gifts that seem more spectacular. Of a piece with this is v. 7: "To each is given a manifestation of the Spirit for the common good." Each is gifted, not merely for private enjoyment but for the common good of all. After this fundamental statement, the list of gifts begins: "To one is given through the Spirit the utterance of wisdom, and to another the utterance of knowledge according to the same Spirit" (12:8).

The utterance of wisdom must be considered in the light of Paul's extended discussion in the first three chapters of this letter, where worldly, wordy wisdom is sharply contrasted with the word of the cross. Therefore it is probable that the utterance of wisdom includes an emphasis on the centrality of the death of Christ in God's dealings with humankind. The word of the cross first evokes trust in Christ and is the necessary word for that trust to continue and to grow; the gospel of the

Crucified is also indispensable for the harmonious working of the body's members for the common good. The Corinthians boast of their wealth of gifts, especially the more spectacular; the cross condemns such boasting. A few sentences before, Paul has reminded his readers of the resurrection confession that the incarnate "Jesus is Lord." The utterance of wisdom is perhaps in the same vein with the implication that the resurrection is to be seen in the light of the cross. Christ's final coming is yet to occur; the Corinthian Christians are not to live as if the end time has arrived. Neither are they free to choose licentiousness or asceticism as their passing fancies dictate. They are freed for a life of faith that knows suffering even as "the Son of man came not to be served but to serve and to give his life as a ransom for many."

Although there is not complete certainty that the utterance of wisdom and the utterance of knowledge must be distinguished, the attempt will be made here to interpret them as distinct in view of the Corinthian situation and Paul's response to it. If the utterance of wisdom emphasizes the indispensability and centrality of Christ's death, it is natural that the utterance of knowledge will include an "obedient and grateful acknowledgement of the deeds and demands of God linked with knowledge of God and what He has done and demands." This knowledge "develops in the life of the Christian as lasting obedience and reflection. For this reason *gnosis* [knowledge] is regarded as a gift of grace which marks the life of the Christian by determining its expression (1 Cor. 1:5; 12:8)."[12] It is knowledge not merely for the sake of knowledge but for the edification of the Christian community. Genuine knowledge is inextricably linked with Christ's concern for the needy neighbor. Ultimately such knowledge is always dependent on being known by God in Jesus Christ.[13] The utterance of wisdom and the utterance of knowledge are, then, complementary: the first emphasizes God's deeds and demands, centering in the cross; the second is a trusting, obedient response to God's works and will which implicitly, at least, encourages a similar response from other members of the body. The two sorts of utterance are inspired by the same Spirit.

There is, of course, the possibility that the utterance of wisdom and the utterance of knowledge are simply the making of terse statements, timely, occasional, Spirit-inspired, proverbial in nature. "A word fitly spoken is like apples of gold in a setting of silver." This interpretation would not negate the importance of the qualifiers "of wisdom" and "of knowledge." An appropriate word might be spoken "one on one," in a council meeting, to those in a small group, or to an assembled congregation.

Tongues and the interpretation of tongues. "To another various kinds of tongues [are given]" (v. 10d). In the Corinthian context, speaking in (various kinds of) tongues is unintelligible, human, Spirit-inspired utterance directed toward God as prayer, praise, thanksgiving. This is not the "speaking in other tongues" reported in Acts 2:1–21. According to Luke, that was not unintelligible; even by unbelievers it was understood. Later in Acts (10:44–48; 19:1–6), the explicit mention of speaking in tongues may refer to the phenomenon of which Paul writes.

Speaking in tongues, or glossolalia, continues to be practiced by human beings all over the globe, both within the church and without. In view of its essentially universal occurrence, we may offer as a general description of glossolalia that it is a panhuman phenomenon consisting in a person's producing consonant and vowel combinations that somewhat resemble ordinary human languages but that, except in matters of beginning, stopping, speed of utterance, and volume, are not under conscious control. Behind a speaking in tongues may be the Holy Spirit, the human spirit, or an evil spirit. The fact that God can use a common human practice (circumcision, baptism, eating and drinking) for special purposes with God's chosen people is once again evident in the Spirit's gift of speaking in tongues.

"To another [is given] the interpretation of tongues" (v. 10e). If some speak in tongues when Christians gather, they must be stopped unless there is someone to interpret, according to Paul. "But if there is no one to interpret, let each of them keep silence in church and speak to himself and to God" (14:28). This is in accordance with the apostle's injunction "Let all things be done for edification." Perhaps from the very nature of the case it is impossible to state whether Paul wanted interpretations to be detailed and precise or simply to give the gist of the glossolalia. And as there were false prophets and false apostles, there were probably also false interpreters of tongues. More recently the story has been told of a meeting where someone pretended to speak in tongues but actually spoke a North American Indian language. An "interpreter" promptly explained the sense—erroneously, according to the speaker.

Nevertheless, since the Spirit-given interpretation of Spirit-inspired

glossolalia edifies the church, tongues and the interpretation of tongues
are significant charisms. An interpreted tongue is of the same worth as
prophecy (14:5). From the evidence it looks as if 1 Corinthians 12—14
was written to the Corinthians because they had a distorted perspective
on the relative importance of the Spirit's gifts. This will become clear
as these three chapters are briefly examined.

In 12:1–3, Paul acknowledges that when the Corinthians were hea-
then, they had experienced such phenomena as speaking in tongues.
The crucial test of a speaking in tongues is what it expresses about
Jesus: "Jesus be cursed!" is not uttered by one speaking by the Spirit
of God, "and no one can say 'Jesus is Lord' except by the Holy Spirit."
At the outset of the discussion on spiritual gifts, then, the apostle
reminds his readers of the Jesus whom they by the Spirit confess as
Lord; Paul places his teaching on the Spirit in a christological setting.

The Corinthian congregation was like congregations today: its members argued with one another. They chose sides among leaders. At the
time of Paul's letter, they were having a tussle over tongues and
prophecy—over which gift is greater. The whole of chapter 14 deals
with this question, and tongues and prophecy are prominent in chapter
13 as well.

Paul's main contention is that all gifts of the Spirit are great; none
is to be despised. Great also is their variety, but they are all from the
same Spirit, Lord, and God. And they are not given for private enjoyment. "To each is given the manifestation of the Spirit for the common
good." Paul lists nine gifts representative of the great variety and num-
bers of charisms. "All these are inspired by one and the same Spirit,
who apportions to each one individually as he wills."

Since all believers are one in Christ, baptized in the Spirit into his
body, no member has a right to say, "Because I am not an eye or ear,
I do not belong to the body." In this way Paul assures those who feel
inferior: each performs an indispensable function. There is also an
admonition to self-styled super-Christians: "The eye cannot say to the
hand nor the head to the feet, 'I have no need of you.' On the contrary,
the parts of the body which seem to be weaker are indispensable."
Believers are all in this together, caring for one another. "If one
member suffers, all suffer together; if one member is honored, all
rejoice together" (12:12–26).

The next paragraph begins in the same vein: "Now you are the body of Christ and individually members of it." But Paul touches his brush to an extended canvas without neglecting the painting he has already accomplished. "And God has appointed in the church first apostles, second prophets, third teachers, then workers of miracles, then healers, helpers, administrators, speakers in various kinds of tongues." The whole people of God, including the local congregation, is involved in this list, which contains helpers and administrators along with apostles and prophets—and speakers in tongues! Again it is a representative list. A further point emphatically made is that there are some gifts that not all members receive. "Not all are apostles, are they?" Not all are prophets, are they? Not all speak in tongues, do they? No! is the decisive answer Paul expects, which at least some of the Corinthians gave and which is the response forthcoming today. The paragraph concludes with the exhortation "But earnestly desire the higher gifts." Among these would be prophecy but not tongues (see 14:1-2).

The short sentence that introduces Paul's chapter on love is difficult to interpret: "And I will show you a still more excellent way" (12:31b). This is generally interpreted as promising either a more excellent way to the higher charisms or a better charism. But to interpret it as promising a better charism is not in keeping with New Testament usage, for love is not designated a charism in the New Testament. It is a fruit of the Spirit, given by God, but not a charism in the technical sense. Thus it seems more likely that Paul is saying only that love is a better way to the higher charisms.

Paul has just urged that his readers "earnestly desire the higher gifts." The apostle evidently thinks this bold encouragement needs to be qualified. *How* shall they seek them? And *which* are the higher gifts? The answer to the first question is primarily in chapter 13 and that to the second mostly in chapter 14. Every Christian is given God's love with the Holy Spirit; responding love is a fruit of the Spirit bestowed on each believer. But believers do not always act in loving ways. Sometimes, as at Corinth, they form factions behind certain leaders and are quarrelsome. In the same city there are those puffed up by knowledge and those who champion glossolalia as a higher gift. "Practicing the Spirit's fruit of love," Paul counsels, "earnestly desire the higher charisms." Because of a loving concern for sister and brother, persons heeding Paul will seek especially those gifts that will upbuild, encourage, and console the congregation as a whole. "Make love your aim and earnestly desire the spiritual gifts, especially that you may prophesy" (1 Cor. 14:1). Caring because of God's loving concern, the believer will earnestly desire the spiritual gifts, especially prophecy, because it does the greatest good for the greatest number of the congregation.

Chapter 13 emphasizes another point that is important for each member of the charismatic congregation: it emphasizes that love is to govern the *use* of the charisms, not merely the seeking of them. As Paul expresses it later, "Let all that you do be done in love." The gifts of the Spirit amount to nothing without love. The fact that love is not so much passive feeling as it is dynamic response and action is clear from vv. 4–7. This paragraph shows some parallels with Gal. 5:22–23, on the fruit of the Spirit. To paraphrase and synthesize these passages, it would not be unfaithful to Paul to say, "The fruit of the Spirit is love, love that rightly rejoices, seeks peace, is patient, kind, good, faithful, gentle, practices self-control, bears, believes, hopes, endures all things." It has often been said that only One comes to mind when this portrait is painted. Interestingly, that One, Jesus, tied loving one's neighbor to doing. After telling one of his best-known parables, the parable of the Good Samaritan, he said to the lawyer, "Go and do likewise."

God's love never ends. The love of those who respond to God in faith and hope also abides. All else is imperfect and transitory, only partially understood till God is seen face to face. "So faith, hope, love abide, these three; but the greatest of these is love."

Probably because the Corinthians have been ranking the gifts, Paul does the same (12:31a), but in the light of how they build up the congregation. His insistence on the indispensability of each member in the body of Christ is fundamental. After teaching that both the seeking and the using of the gifts are to be motivated by love, the apostle moves on in chapter 14 to show why prophecy is a higher, and tongues a lower, gift.

The reason for glossolalia's being ranked as a lower gift is that when one speaks in tongues, "no one understands him" (1 Cor. 14:2), whereas "he who prophesies speaks to men for their upbuilding and encouragement and consolation" (14:3). It is noteworthy also that according to Paul, glossolalia is not proclamation to people but prayer to God: "For one who speaks in a tongue speaks not to men but to God" (14:2).

Since each person is significant, it is relatively important that "he who speaks in a tongue edifies himself" (v. 4), but prophecy is greater than tongues because "he who prophesies edifies the church" (v. 4). Supportive of tongues, Paul does not want the good supplanting the best: "Now I want you all to speak in tongues, but even more to prophesy" (v. 5). He again ranks prophecy over tongues unless the speaking in tongues is interpreted: "He who prophesies is greater than he who speaks in tongues, unless some one interprets, so that the church may be edified" (v. 5). When interpreted, tongues edify the congregation and they rank on a par with prophecy, but they are not identical to prophecy, since glossolalia is prayer to God, according to Paul.

Since uninterpreted tongues do not communicate, they do not edify others; that is the point Paul reemphasizes in the next paragraph, closing it with an implicit admonition to employ the higher gifts: "Since you are eager for manifestations of the Spirit, strive to excel in building up the church" (v. 12).

The seriousness of Paul's counsel for the service of worship becomes even more obvious as he continues. If a tongue is not interpreted, not everyone can say amen to the glossolalist's thanksgiving; the utterance is not understood and is, therefore, unedifying (vv. 13–17). Paul then bursts forth in a bit of the "boasting" rather common in the Corinthian epistles, a boasting quickly qualified, however: "I thank God that I speak in tongues more than you all; nevertheless, in church I would rather speak five words with my mind, in order to instruct others, than ten thousand words in a tongue" (v. 18). As an evangelist used to ask in relation to this passage, "What kind of odds do you want?"

Is there a hint, as the next paragraph begins, that glossolalia is a gift more appropriate for "babes in Christ" than for more mature believers? Paul writes, "Brethren, do not be children in your thinking; be babes in evil, but in thinking be mature" (v. 20; see also 13:11: "When I was a child . . ."). In this connection it is significant to note that the instances of speaking in tongues in Acts are all in the context of the *initial* revelation to the persons involved that Jesus is *Lord*. Is it that when the fact that Jesus the crucified is Lord is really driven home to people by the Spirit of God, one natural response is to speak the unspeakable? It may be, however, that in this passage (14:20), Paul is simply chiding the Corinthians for childishness in their lofty evaluation of tongues or in their undisciplined, uncaring use of them.

In the remainder of this paragraph it seems at first as if Paul is inconsistent in his discussion of tongues and prophecy in relation to believers and unbelievers. In the passage from Isaiah (v. 21), God is quoted as saying that his people will not listen to him when he speaks to them by men of strange tongues. But on the basis of this Paul goes on, "Thus, tongues are a sign not for believers but for unbelievers" (v. 22). Apparently reversing his field, he states that if outsiders or unbelievers hear a whole congregation speaking in tongues, they will say the members are mad, but if all members prophesy, an unbeliever will be convicted, worship God, and declare God to be really among them (vv. 23–25).

For this apparent inconsistency, Krister Stendahl suggests a succinct and satisfactory solution. He suggests that Paul here uses the word "sign" with a negative connotation, as equivalent to "mere sign." A mere sign does not lead unbelievers to faith but leads them to the hardening of unbelief. For believers, glossolalia is not a sign but part of their experience. But unbelievers need intelligible prophecy of God's word for repentance and faith.[14]

Paul never rebukes the Corinthians for dullness. If it is sinful to bore a worshiper, the Corinthian congregation must have been blameless in at least one regard. Rather, when the members assembled, each was bubbling over with a hymn, a lesson, a revelation, a tongue, or an interpretation. Paul counsels, "Let all things be done for edification" (v. 26). He evidently does not assume there will always be glossolalia in the gathered community, for he writes, "If any speak in a tongue . . ." There are to be only two, at most three, speaking thus, and in turn, with someone to interpret; without interpretation there must be no glossolalia in church but only privately in prayer to God. In keeping with Paul's general evaluation of prophecy and tongues, he assumes that prophecy will be central in worship; there is no conditional clause such as "If anyone prophesies" but rather the command "Let two or three prophets speak . . ."

In the last paragraph, dealing with tongues, Paul "pulls rank"—apostolic rank—a gift from Jesus Christ, Lord. What he is writing is a "command of the Lord," and anyone not honoring this is not to be recognized as an authentic prophet. Paul writes specifically about prophecy and tongues: "So, my brethren, earnestly desire to prophesy, and do not forbid speaking in tongues; but all things should be done decently and in order" (vv. 37–40).

It is obvious that chapters 12—14 of Corinthians were evoked primarily by sharp disagreements concerning tongue speaking in the Corinthian congregation; otherwise Paul would not have needed to spend so much time on it, especially during the last part of this section. It is significant that anything positive the apostle says about tongues has a qualification or caution attached (12:31; 14:1–5, 18–19).

It is time to lay to rest the idea that those speaking in tongues in our land are primarily the psychologically weak and crippled. There may have been a time, decades ago, when there was some evidence for this. The contemporary anthropologist Felicitas Goodman puts the shoe on the other foot: "In doing work in this country, anthropologists have found the following interesting fact: When they compared carefully chosen groups of worshipers that were only distinguished by one group speaking in tongues and the other not, the tongue speakers had the better mental health."[15] Whether this is always so or not is perhaps not very significant; what is important is to realize the comparative uselessness of debate on these grounds.

In the second place, it seems quite fruitless to argue whether one who speaks in tongues is speaking an actual human language. What difference does it make? At any rate, the glossolalia that Paul describes was unintelligible; to edify, it needed interpretation. That those hearing one speaking in tongues have occasionally heard an English, German, or Latin word or phrase is possible. Again Goodman has a relevant comment. She points out that language builds hundreds of thousands of words from probably fewer than eighty different sounds shared by all humans. Purely statistically, a combination of sounds in "tongues" is likely to be a word in *some* language. "But the whole phrase is not usually a meaningful sentence, given in a shared code, as we understand this in ordinary language."[16] Further, scientific linguistic analysis has shown that the structural features of thousands of languages, contemporary and ancient, do not correspond with those of tongue-speaking utterances. But this is a matter for continuing scientific inquiry, subject to the evidence uncovered.

Third, does it seem best for the body of Christ that glossolalists remain to share their gifts in their original congregations (many of which may be small, struggling rural or inner-city churches) or that they leave and concentrate by the hundreds or thousands with those of like mind in the suburbs or outer city? It seems most salutary for our congregation that those who speak in tongues remain among us. They would be missed very much.

Fourth, a serious stumbling block to harmony between Christians in charismatic renewal and other Christians in renewal is the use of the term "baptism in the Spirit." Since Pentecost, believers have held there is one baptism, baptism in the name of the Father, Son, and Holy Spirit into Christ's body (see Acts 2:37–42; Eph. 4:4–6). Baptism without the Spirit is merely something ranging from a sprinkling to a bath. There is no baptized believer without the Spirit. Is it possible for all Christians to agree that every Christian baptism is a baptism in the Spirit? Is it possible to agree further that after baptism in the Spirit, believers' lives can be renewed by being filled with the Spirit? If we can agree on matters such as these, it would be highly significant. If we cannot, renewal in the church itself may be severely compromised.

Over two decades ago a colleague returned from a city in a western state with many questions about his experience with a congregational prayer group there. A "prophetess" had uttered oracles in King James English about the history and prehistory of our country. There had been speaking in tongues. The "prophetess" was not impressive. What should be made of glossolalists—in a main-line church?!

Most responses to such events were negative in those days. Perhaps that was inevitable. If Christians with a charismatic experience describe it in terms of classical Pentecostal theology, they become alienated from their own Christian community unless they are Pentecostals.[17]

Surely from the earliest days there have been incidents for which many of us need to repent. People of various persuasions have suffered deep pain from ruptured relationships, family rifts, and congregational splits caused by the experience and use of tongues. Is anyone qualified to cast the first stone about the past or the present? But there is a different, more open spirit abroad now.

It is widely acknowledged that the neo-Pentecostal movement is instrumental in the continuing renewal of the Christian church. Krister Stendahl could write as early as 1976 that glossolalists and those not speaking in tongues need each other "if the church is to receive and express the fullness of the Christian life."[18]

Through the glossolalists' unintelligible prayer to God, the glossolalists themselves are edified, and if their speaking is interpreted, those hearing the interpretation are also built up, as Paul testifies.

Speakers in tongues witness that with their gifts come a deepened reverence for Jesus Christ as Lord, a hunger for the Scriptures, and a deepened love for people.

It must have been rather early in the sixties when Mary, a good neighbor and friend, received the gift of tongues. Perhaps only a few of us in our congregation were aware of it, and that seemed as it should be. Mary carried on in her quiet Christian way, a real blessing in our church. Perhaps fifteen years after she received the gift, she mentioned it casually and naturally one Sunday, because of the content of a Bible study in our parish hall. A few others in our congregation are known to speak in tongues—there may be many. At any rate, they do not "blaze abroad the matter" but go about being effective, esteemed members of Christ's body along with those otherwise gifted. "How good and pleasant it is when sisters and brothers dwell in unity!" And how sad it is when brothers and sisters seethe in disharmony, as in the church at Corinth and in many since!

Stendahl has the "conviction that the question of glossolalia in the churches is a pastoral one."[19] Will a pastor understand when a parishioner has had a deep experience of renewal, with tongues or without? Will he or she respond negatively, with some such remark as, "Tom, you didn't need a thing. You have been baptized. You've always been a Christian." This may be true; God alone is the heart knower. The Christians at Rome had been baptized; yet Paul appealed to them, "Present your bodies a living sacrifice . . . acceptable to God." The Corinthian Christians had been baptized; Paul beseeched them, "Be reconciled to God," and he wrote to them that the Macedonian Christians first "gave themselves to the Lord" before they gave beyond their means to the Jerusalem disciples. Yes, the question is a pastoral one. Can pastor and people work harmoniously regardless of the presence or absence of the more spectacular gifts?

Out of the blue a college friend dropped into a professor's office one day. After a time he mentioned that he and his wife Ruby were members of a congregation where the pastor and many of the people spoke in tongues. "Ruby and I do not speak in tongues," he said, "but we feel welcome there. We sense no pressure on us to strive for this gift." Wise pastor and people!

Finally, how might Paul respond to our situation today? Perhaps he would say, "Tertius, take a letter: 'Paul an apostle of Christ Jesus to all churches on the planet—Grace and peace! All we Christians are one body. We are all charismatic. All of us greatly need one another.' "

Gifts of Serving

Although all charisms might be considered under the heading of serving (cf. 1 Cor. 12:5; Eph. 4:11–12), it is also possible to distinguish between gifts of speaking and gifts of serving. Nevertheless, all gifts are intended to "serve" for the common good.

Serving. The basic meaning of *diakonia,* the New Testament word for "serving," is "waiting at table." This was Martha's activity when she became "distraught from much serving." The occasion for the choosing of Stephen and six others "to serve tables" was the "daily serving" (Acts 6:1–2). At this very time the Twelve said, "But we will devote ourselves to prayer and the ministry [*diakonia*] of the word." According to a large body of opinion, it is probable that "the original meaning is reflected in this phrase. The Word of God is offered as the bread of life."[20]

But the meaning of serving has been extended to cover "any 'discharge of service' in genuine love."[21] In Rom. 12:6–7, Paul writes, "Having gifts that differ according to the grace given us, let us use them: . . . if service, in our serving."

Serving is given depth of meaning in the New Testament by Jesus himself. "For which is the greater," he asks, "one who sits at table, or one who serves? Is it not the one who sits at table? But I am among you as one who serves" (Luke 22:27). In a parallel passage in Mark, Jesus says, "For the Son of man also came not to be served but to serve, and to give his life a ransom for many" (10:45). In these contexts, Jesus is making service decisive for discipleship as well as for his own mission. In his parable of the last judgment (Matt. 25:31–46), Jesus mentions the kinds of serving those who are cursed neglect: giving food and drink to the hungry and thirsty, welcoming strangers, clothing the naked, visiting the sick and imprisoned. He adds, "As you did it not to one of the least of these, you did it not to me." It is highly significant that neither the blessed nor the cursed realized what they had been doing or neglecting: "Lord, when did we see thee hungry?" The disciple is not keeping score. "The fruit of the Spirit *is* love, . . . kindness, goodness."

Serving, then, is genuine love acting for others. Through the Holy Spirit God has poured his love into our hearts. God and others "we love because he first loved us."

Helping. There is a distinctive picture in the roots of the word for "helping" in the Greek. In 1 Cor. 12:18 it is usually translated "helpers" to make it consistent with the other personal terms, but it could be translated more literally as "helping acts." In accordance with the roots involved, it might be rendered as "taking hold of," either in place of or in behalf of another. Helping is giving a hand to the task at hand.

"It was simply there before us and needed to be done," said Vic Stevens of a church in Parma Heights, Ohio. Vic coordinates the refugee ministry of his congregation. He described a type of situation involved in the kind of helping that is "taking hold," which is exactly what happened. Not only have Vietnamese and Laotian families been sponsored since the late seventies but, beginning in 1983, a Czechoslovakian family has been helped, the Juneks, Jerry and his wife, Lou, and their two-year-old daughter, Linda. Aid was given to find them an apartment, and a call went out during a Sunday service for an interpreter and English teacher. Joe Novak, retired, who had come from Czechoslovakia years before, volunteered, "coming out of retirement" to give expert help. "God always sends the right volunteers" the congregation has discovered. Not only did Joe teach the family English but he also taught them survival skills like shopping and handling money. Presently another member offered Jerry a night cleaning job that he was glad to have till he secured a position in his field as an electrical apprentice.[22] Helping is a way to "dream globally, take hold locally." God's Spirit brings together helpers and those to be helped.

Administering. If a picture of a man or woman in a dark pin-striped suit in an office suite comes into the mind's eye when "administrators" is read in 1 Cor. 12:28, a "reversed vision" is needed. Paul is using a word that originally meant "steering a ship," the "art of the helmsman." In the congregation, leading, guiding, steering are needed and provided.

A Lutheran leader, no longer living, himself something like Peter, used to say occasionally, "When the Twelve ate together, wherever Peter sat was the head of the table." Perhaps he was right. At any rate, in the pre-Pentecost days "Peter stood up among the brethren" and led them in choosing a replacement for Judas. It is Peter who preached the Pentecost sermon, answered the Jewish high court, spoke at the Jerusalem conference and stood out generally in the first part of Acts. But James (the Lord's brother) seems to have had the last and decisive word at the Jerusalem conference; he was an apostle and became a prominent leader in the earliest church. Along with Peter, the other apostles should be mentioned as administrators, as well as the Jerusalem seven, who were chosen to administer the distribution of food for the congregation. The elders who are linked with the apostles as leaders in the congregation at Jerusalem should also be included among the administrators. It is likely that those Paul addresses as bishops and deacons in his Letter to the Philippians (1:1) are also exercising the gift of helmsmanship. But the majority of the acting congregational leaders in the early church remain relatively unknown.

Leadership is vitally necessary for a congregation to function in the body of Christ, just as it is necessary to a secular state. And if God grasped and guided King Cyrus to do the will of a God he did not know (Isa. 45:1–6), surely God grasps and girds certain Christians to exercise leadership in congregations. From the context it seems that any person may be elected to exercise leadership and that the criterion for the charismatic in this area and others is not the function itself but whether it is employed with the Spirit's guidance "for the common good."

Not long ago in an ecumenical setting near Bethlehem, two Roman Catholic priests were telling of tongue-speaking groups in their parishes. One spoke in derogatory terms. He had had very little to do with those involved. The other said that although he himself was not a glossolalist, he had been with the group frequently, almost from its inception, trying to curb, encourage, understand, and guide the members when necessary. The members had caused no difficulties; in fact, he added, when he needed people to undertake tough tasks in his parish, he knew he could count on them. It seemed to the hearers that the second priest had been exercising his leadership more charismatically, more "for the common good."

The question may be raised why Paul mentions leadership in almost the same breath as apostles, prophets, and evangelists. It is because he insists, on the one hand, that all believers are charismatic and on the other, that there must be order, not confusion, so that the worship of God may be edifying. With responsible leadership, what might have been mere noise can be transformed into a succession of charisms exercised for the common good. This kind of guidance is vital not only in ordering a service of worship but also in directing all aspects of life in the church.

The gift of administration is a composite. Men and women who skillfully lead their churches and church-owned or church-related institutions are extraordinarily versatile gifts from God.

Contributing. Three final gifts are listed in Rom. 12:6-8. The phrases "in liberality," "with zeal," and "with cheerfulness" stress the style and manner in which the charisms of, respectively, contributing, caring, and showing mercy are to be used in the body of Christ. It is likely that the three phrases point to constant needs in the Christian community which every believer from time to time is qualified and prompted to meet.

Some members of the congregation may hold substantial assets or have a large income. "Let such a person," exhorts Paul, "share in liberality." Another possible translation is "Let him who shares do it with simplicity [i.e., without ulterior motives]." There are pitfalls for both donor and receiver. Judaism recognized this by making it possible for the poor to receive gifts in secret without having to confront the donors. Saint Vincent de Paul in the seventeenth century started a slum mission in France for the care of prisoners, the sick, the abjectly poor. He is quoted as saying to the sister attending him at the point of death, "Sister, we must love these people very much, so that they can forgive us for having helped them."[23]

Some congregations today have special gifts and opportunities "to contribute with liberality."

As a part of a twentieth-birthday celebration, one church voted a Project Gratitude, a campaign to raise a gift of at least one hundred thousand dollars for a mission-partner congregation.

One couple gave the church $650,000, which proved to be an impetus gift for a new sanctuary.[24] For some couples, giving $650 might involve more of a sacrifice than giving $650,000 would involve for others. To each person, however, the Spirit gives a gift of contributing; as every gift, it shrivels away unless exercised.

Caring. Although the phrase in Rom. 12:8c may be translated "he who gives aid, with zeal," this does not present the whole picture. The basic meaning of the verb is "to be first, to preside, to lead." But in the Pauline letters, where all instances of this word in the New Testament occur, there is the associated sense of "to care for." The explanation lies in the "fact that caring was the obligation of the leading members of the infant church."[25] The contexts in general show that a verb with a more inclusive meaning is preferable here and that the phrase might better be translated "he who cares, with zeal."

When Joanne and John Jenssen heard in church in Portland, Maine, that there were some "unaccompanied minors" among Cambodian refugees needing resettlement, their response was swift. "My husband and I prayed about it," says Joanne, "and decided we had the room. . . . So we put in for two." Two boys, Kouk and Vong, both in their late teens, now have a new life in a new land.

Although nothing that Joanne does really surprises the members of her church, they cannot help being amazed at the scope and intensity of her activities. She sings in the choirs, teaches English to Southeast Asian refugees, teaches a Sunday-school class, leads a Bible study, and continues to be the church treasurer. In addition she works with terminally ill cancer patients.

For fifteen years she has known she has multiple sclerosis. Having been up and down from the disease, she says, "Right now, I am doing more than my neurologist said I can do, but that's because the Lord is doing it. . . . The more I read Scripture, the more the Lord says, 'Go!' "[26] Here is someone who has received the gift of caring with intensive zeal while humbly acknowledging the source of the gift and of the energy to exercise it.

Showing Mercy. The words of Rom. 12:8d are "he who does acts of mercy, with cheerfulness." If mercy is shown dourly and sourly, even passively, much of the blessing can evaporate. But if acts of mercy are performed gladly and buoyantly, praise to God can burst forth. "The quality of mercy is not strained"—it is mirthfully spontaneous when

Christ's Spirit inhabits and empowers the believer's faith. The Good Samaritan proves himself a neighbor by showing mercy on the one who has been robbed, beaten, and left half dead. God's mercy in Christ flows through grateful believers to those needing mercy and cheer.

A Christian nurse at Fairview Hospital, Minneapolis, detected the backache of one who had been lying in bed several days since surgery. "Want a back rub?" she asked cheerily. Scarcely giving the patient time to answer, she deftly helped him turn over, and her strong, tender, warm hands went to work. The quality of her mercy was not strained.

During the Great Depression three thrifty ladies of modest means considered the plight of their sister Mary, her husband, and the couple's five children. Said the leader of the trio, "One of Mary's children is going to go to my alma mater." They had already helped Mary's oldest daughter graduate from nurses' training and her next to oldest daughter from junior college. The three sisters were happy in their aggressively merciful giving and interest-free lending. It was not necessary to go begging to them; they came to you, enthusiastic, eyes aglow, ready to help. The vocational preparation of five nieces and nephews and the well-being of an entire family depended on the cheerful mercies of these three sisters, dedicated to Christ and his people.

Healing. "To another [are given] gifts of healing by the one Spirit" (1 Cor. 12:9b). The people of God have always been confident that the Lord is their healer from sin and sickness and death, and just as confident that the Lord is their healer *in* sin and sickness and death: the believer is liberated from the guilt and power of sin yet is still a sinner; the believer is more or less healthy but will die, and may or may not die "healthy."

In Jesus a fresh surge of God's ruling power pervaded the world. Through Jesus' proclamation of God's reign, God's reign came, replacing fear with faith, guilt with forgiveness, sickness with health. But Jesus did not heal all the sick millions of his time, not even all the sick in Judea, Samaria, and Galilee. He gave his life for the ultimate and total wholeness of the entire world. "In Christ God was reconciling the world to himself, not counting their trespasses against them."

Out of compassion, he healed, sometimes in response to faith but also to give indicators of the inception through himself of God's kingdom. He died and rose and commissioned apostles to make disciples of all nations, baptizing and teaching the observance of everything he had commanded. On Pentecost he founded a caring community in Jerusalem that carried on his ministry of preaching, teaching, and healing. Through his servants he founded other such congregations in other areas. Not everyone who heard the gospel believed, and not every sick believer who prayed or was prayed for was healed (2 Cor. 12:8–10). But some did believe and some were healed!

It is still so. Some do believe. Some are healed, whether through their own faith or the faith of concerned others or simply because the Lord wills to give a special sign of God's gracious reign. In all this there is mystery that can nourish trust and humility. It was once estimated by a medical doctor that of those afflicted with cancer, one in twenty experiences a healing that cannot be foreseen or explained by medical science.

God alone heals, and among the people of God there is a climate of healing as they call on the Lord for health and salvation. Sometimes God raises up in the congregation a "healing sort of person," one who has "gifts of healing," and extraordinary things happen. Sometimes the healings can be documented as falling outside the capacity of current science to explain. Sometimes they cannot be so documented. The therapeutic power of the forgiveness of sins for the total person can scarcely be measured. When we remember baptism and when we share the Supper, our crucified and risen Lord Jesus Christ can give powerful "preventive medicine" and "invigorating vitamins." And all the while, God is sustaining, restoring, and improving our health through the agency of physical-education instructors, teachers of health and hygiene, nurses, physicians and surgeons, fathers and mothers, and sisters and brothers. For all this, God is to be praised. God is to be praised also for those unpredictable times when, acting through one person, a group, or some other intermediary, the Spirit swoops down like a gull, heals, and soars on. God's church has confidence that wherever and whenever God's reign in Christ is proclaimed, there and then the sun of righteousness is rising, with healing on his wings.

One day in a city of the Far West, two Lutheran pastors from the Midwest were leading a week of evangelical outreach. The wife of the pastor of one of the churches involved had suffered for some years from multiple sclerosis. One of the visiting pastors was prompted to say to the husband of the sick woman, "Let's go and pray that your wife may be healed." The husband, another local pastor, and the two visitors did just that. Almost immediately there were healing changes in the wife, in her feet, in her face, in her walk, and otherwise; the transformation was perceived not only by her but presently by her husband, family, doctor, nurse, hairdresser, and others. Years later her healing was reaffirmed to this writer by her son, who reported that she was still in good health.

In this instance, whose was the gift of healing? It was *God's* gift to God's praying children. It was special for the wife and her husband— and a gift for the three other pastors as well. Although most consider "To another [are given] gifts of healing" to refer to a healer in the church rather than the one healed, some take the gift of healing to refer to those who are healed. The charisms are given to the church for the benefit of all.

Christ's great commission is to "make disciples of all nations." Although there is no specific command by the risen Lord to heal, the church from the beginning has been concerned for its members' wholeness of body and mind. Believers are encouraged to pray in faith for healing. How or whether there is healing in a particular instance is for God to determine. Lack of healing must not be attributed to a lack of faith. Imagine the increased hurt experienced by a victim of multiple sclerosis when some of her "friends" (who were not even members of her church) told her that she remained sick simply because she did not have the faith to be healed! Paul had faith to be healed, but his "thorn in the flesh" persisted. Yet God's grace sufficed. Not all petitions are granted, but all prayers are heard. God is love.

Miracles. "To another [is given] the working of miracles" (1 Cor. 12:10a). Jesus himself was "mighty in deed and word." He performed the miracle of evoking a saving faith in God. He forgave sinners and stilled a storm, and he fed thousands with a few loaves and fish. To a father who confessed both his belief and unbelief he said, "All things are possible to him who believes." Through faith, "the believer shares in the rule of God and therefore, either actively or passively, experiences miraculous power."[27]

It is then no surprise that Jesus promised his disciples that they would carry on his mission with the miraculous power of his Spirit: "I send the promise of my Father upon you; but stay in the city, until you are clothed with power from on high" (Luke 24:49). The Book of Acts records that Christ's disciples also were mighty in deed and word. Peter proclaimed the Gospel on Pentecost and three thousand were converted. While John and Peter were going up to the temple, they were met by a man blind from birth seeking alms. Peter had no money but said, "In the name of Jesus Christ of Nazareth, walk." Peter took his right hand, raised him, and he was soon walking, leaping, and praising God. The apostles made very clear to the crowd that it was not by their own power or piety that the lame man leaped but by the name of Jesus and faith in his name (Acts 3:1-16). By the same "dynamite" (Greek, *dynamis*), the apostles gave their verbal witness to the resurrection: "And with great power the apostles gave their testimony to the resurrection of the Lord Jesus, and great grace was upon them all" (Acts 4:33).

Contending that the Spirit comes not by works of the law but through the gospel heard with faith, Paul asks the "foolish Galatians," "Does he who supplies the Spirit to you and works miracles among you do so by works of the law, or by hearing with faith?" (Gal. 3:5). The implication is that supplying the Spirit and working miracles are inextricably joined in God's economy for congregations.

In the same chapter in which Paul claims his apostolic credentials (2 Cor. 12:12), he teaches that God's miraculous power functions as a companion to human weakness. Having just mentioned his "thorn in the flesh," Paul writes,

> Three times I besought the Lord about this, that it should leave me; but he said to me, "My grace is sufficient for you, for my power is made perfect in weakness." I will all the more gladly boast of my weaknesses, that the power of Christ may rest upon me. For the sake of Christ, then, I am content with weaknesses, insults, hardships, persecutions, and calamities; for when I am weak, then I am strong. (2 Cor. 12:8-10)

A miracle may take the shape of an immediate or gradual healing of body or mind, or it may assume the form of grace that is enough to sustain a miracle faith in a weak person whose "thorn" is not removed, a person weak enough to share in faith the omnipotence of God.

Faith. "To another [is given] faith by the same Spirit" (1 Cor. 12:9a). The faith Paul means here is not that which is the indispensable core of every Christian life, for he is speaking of a gift granted to some believers and not to others. Nor is it the faith or faithfulness that is the fruit of the Spirit, for in each believer the Spirit is producing fruit. The fruit of the Spirit is love, joy, faithfulness (Gal. 5:22–23). The faith Paul means is heroic faith, a mountain-moving confidence (1 Cor. 13:2) in God whose power is miraculous. It is the kind of trust the Syrophoenician woman had. She "caught Jesus in his own words" (Luther). Not put off by the inference that Gentiles were dogs, she pressed for some doggie crumbs from the master's table. She would not abate her petitions for her demon-possessed daughter. Jesus said, "O woman, great is your faith! Be it done for you as you desire." Then "her daughter was healed instantly" (Matt. 15:21–28). Such a faith in God Abraham was given when he believed that Sarah and he would have a son in spite of her age and barrenness and his own body as good as dead. The old man was "fully convinced that God was able to do what he had promised" (Rom. 4:19–21).

Obviously there is a close connection between this faith and "gifts of healing" and "miracles." "Faith" is the general term; it manifests itself in healing and other miracles wrought by God.

Healing, miracles, and faith seem to point in a special way to a God who hears prayers and in whose loving will things happen that cannot be explained on the basis of the natural course of events. The greatest miracles are the creation, Jesus' incarnation, crucifixion, and resurrection, and what God does for the universe through all this.

Has God ceased performing miracles? Does God still make the incredible credible, evoking trust in Christ? Is that miracle? Are there healings and other things taking place, when a few Christians or many have prayed, that cannot be explained on the basis of natural causes? Are these miracles? Somehow most Christians seem convinced that the God of the big miracles cares also about the healing of a person with cancer as well as the flight and the fall of a sparrow.

A young Christian scholar was trying to earn an advanced university degree. A certain professor, Dr. Harmon, was doing all he could to throw up roadblocks. He really had nothing against the degree candidate. He did hate Professor Fletcher, however, and Fletcher was the young scholar's adviser. Fletcher had been brought in from another university to chair the department, though everyone knew that Harmon wanted the appointment. The hatred was mutual. When Fletcher died of heart complications, his mother exclaimed, "Dr. Harmon killed my boy."

The student got a new adviser, but Harmon, still filled with hatred, kept opposing the young man's candidacy. He was against the dissertation topic; it had been suggested by Fletcher! Outvoted by the department, Harmon was still unhappy. The last weeks of the crucial school year were approaching. The dissertation had been written, typed, and bound. Written examinations had been taken and passed. Remaining were the oral exam and the public defense of the dissertation. What would Harmon do now?

The day for the orals arrived. All the professors were there, except Harmon. The hours passed, the exam was over, Harmon had not shown. Because of a mix-up, Harmon had been at home sleeping during the time of the examination. The day for the public defense of the dissertation came. It was to be held in a historic chamber of the oldest building on campus, a more festive setting than an ordinary seminar room. All arrived on time, including professors from other departments—except Harmon. He never showed up at all. Afterwards it was ascertained that a legitimate reason kept him from meeting his appointments that day. God still works miracles, and for the young scholar this was surely one of them.

Distinguishing between spirits. "To another [is given] the ability to distinguish between spirits" (1 Cor. 12:10c). Since this follows immediately after the reference to prophecy, "spirits" means "spirits of prophets." This is confirmed by Paul's statement in 1 Cor. 14:32: "The spirits of prophets are subject to prophets." Similar language is found in 1 John: "Test the spirits . . . for many false prophets have gone out into the world."

Jesus' perceptiveness in distinguishing between spirits is recorded in the Gospels. Though demoniacs addressed him as Holy One of God and Son of the Most High God, Jesus refused such testimony and cast out the unclean spirits. Although Peter had just confessed Jesus to be the Messiah, he was resoundingly rebuked when he undertook to block his Master's way to death on a cross: "Get behind me, Satan! For you are not on the side of God, but of men" (Mark 8:33). Whatever is merely human descends to the demonic when diametrically opposed to

God. Jesus warned of false prophets, saying, "By their fruits you will know them."

The apostle Paul was himself a prophet and a discerner of spirits. Like his Master, he refused testimony, though true, from a demoniac and freed a spirit-possessed slave girl from her affliction (Acts 16:16–18). Paul also had to rebuke the apostle Peter when his hypocritical actions at Antioch did not square with the truth of the gospel but rather implied a "false gospel," forgiveness by works of law. Paul's response was immediate, thorough, appropriate.

The scriptural evidence and other evidence from the early church show that there were several ways that the gift of discerning between spirits was manifested. First, the gift could result in decisive on-the-spot action against words or deeds that tended to falsify and pervert the gospel and therefore to hinder and thwart the mission of Christ's church. Second, while someone was prophesying in the context of a service of worship, others were to weigh what was being said, presumably with the purpose of evaluating it for its authenticity, relevance, and power for edifying those listening. Third, as time went on there was opportunity for the church to make a more studied response to false prophets and false prophecy. This is reflected in some New Testament books written some decades after 1 Corinthians. The First Letter to Timothy reflects a situation of unsound doctrine and practice: "Now the Spirit expressly says that in later times some will depart from the faith by giving heed to deceitful spirits and doctrines of demons" (4:1). First John is more specific and positive in its criterion for judging spirits and prophecy true or false: "Beloved, do not believe every spirit, but test the spirits to see whether they are of God; for many false prophets have gone out into the world. By this you know the Spirit of God: every spirit which confesses that Jesus Christ has come in the flesh is of God, and every spirit which does not confess Jesus is not of God. This is the spirit of antichrist, of which you heard that it was coming, and now it is in the world already" (4:1–3).

The apostle Paul could hardly emphasize sufficiently the prime importance of the Spirit's gift of prophecy for the building-up and encouragement and consolation of the church (1 Cor. 14:1–5). Earlier he had exhorted, "Do not quench the Spirit, do not despise prophesying, but test everything; hold fast what is good" (1 Thess. 5:19–20). Because the Holy Spirit must not be *extinguished* in and among believers, the spirits must be *distinguished*. Confident that Christ had commissioned him an apostle of God's good news in Jesus, Paul would brook no foolishness from would-be prophets who challenged his gospel or his apostleship. With cutting satire he addressed those in Corinth who might resist him and his message: "What! Did the word of God originate with you, or are you the only ones it has reached? If any one thinks that he is a prophet, or spiritual, he should acknowledge that what I am writing to you is a command of the Lord. If anyone does not recognize this, he is not recognized" (1 Cor. 14:36–38).

In his mercy, God's Spirit has preserved into our times the apostolic testimony to Jesus Christ Lord. All prophecy, proclamation, and teaching are evaluated with him and his gospel as the touchstone. Just as the functions of prophets came to be performed more and more by officials of the congregation when the gospels, Paul's epistles, and the other New Testament books came to be regarded as Scripture, so the distinguishing between spirits of prophets tended to be practiced with reference to the recorded Word.

God's Spirit is sovereign and may choose to give the gift of inspired speech today, as well as the gift of immediate discernment, just as in the primitive church. It is claimed in our day that sometimes when Christians assemble there are persons who sense by the Holy Spirit that there is an alien spirit at work and who proceed to resist or exorcise it. The experience of most of us in distinguishing between spirits is probably not of this sort.

On the ecumenical scene there is a "distinguishing between spirits" in the constitutional basis of the World Council of Churches: "The World Council of Churches is a fellowship of churches which confess the Lord Jesus Christ as God and Savior *according to the Scriptures*."[28] Some groups that claim to be churches are not eligible for WCC membership because they do not subscribe to this constitutional basis.

6

The Spirit's Fruit for All Christians

The Christians at Corinth were a gifted lot. At the same time, they were troubled with factionalism, jealousy, incest, marriage problems, disrespect for the Eucharist, false doctrine, pride, and the like. Paul did not disparage their giftedness but reproached their immaturity and fleshliness.

Learning from his Lord, Paul had a way of putting things into perspective. As he began his discussion of spiritual gifts (1 Corinthians 12—14), he pointed to the fundamental gift from God's Holy Spirit: faith that confesses, "Jesus is Lord." In the midst of his discourse on gifts of the Spirit he indicated that without the fruit of God's Spirit that is love, the charisms tend to render their recipients noisy nothings, gaining nothing. "Make love your aim, and earnestly desire the spiritual gifts, especially that you may prophesy," exhorts Paul. Making love one's aim results primarily in earnestly desiring to prophesy, for those who prophesy are concerned not merely for their own edification but for that of others also, speaking to people "for their upbuilding and encouragement and consolation."

It is elsewhere in Paul that we learn that love is a *fruit* of the Spirit: "The fruit of the Spirit is love, joy, peace, patience, kindness, goodness, faithfulness, gentleness, self-control" (Gal. 5:22–23). It is *not* a human work but a *fruit of the Spirit,* produced by God.

Inevitable, the Fruit of the Spirit

Love is the inevitable fruit of the Spirit. It is an inevitable result not because we feel its stirrings (can we always be sure of these feelings?)

nor even because we observe it in others (again, are we certain they act out of *love?*). Rather, it is a sure product of the Spirit because God's Word so teaches. Paul does not write, "The fruit of the Spirit *ought to be* love." He writes, "The fruit of the Spirit *is* love."

Paul expresses the same fact in a different way in an earlier verse of Galatians 5. In a verse that summarizes Galatians and to some extent Paul's whole theology, the apostle writes, "For in Christ Jesus neither circumcision nor uncircumcision is of any avail, but faith working through love" (v. 6). That is, in Christianity neither works nor lack of them counts for salvation, but faith working through love. We are saved through faith because of Christ; that faith works through love. As Luther said, we are saved by faith alone—but faith is never alone.

Although faith and love are inseparable they can, of course, be distinguished. It is necessary and profitable to distinguish between them theologically, but not chronologically. To paraphrase Luther, before faith asks, "What shall I do?" it is already off and away, working through love.

If love is the inevitable fruit of the Spirit, what happened in Corinth? From the evidence it looks as if the Corinthians were ceasing to concentrate on "Jesus Christ and him crucified," the indispensable foundation. The Corinthians were glorying in Paul or Apollos or Peter or perhaps a "spiritual" Christ rather than in the historical Jesus Christ crucified. Tending to forget that "to each is given the manifestation of the Spirit for the common good," every individual was glorying in a gift as if it were not a trust for the sake of caring for each member of Christ's body. To renew the Corinthians in faith and fruit, Paul focused on the one indispensable gift, Jesus Christ crucified. It is his portrait we are to see in 1 Corinthians 13. A meaningful way to interpret the text on the fruit of the Spirit in Galatians is in the light of 1 Corinthians 13 and the life, death, and resurrection of Jesus.

First, the context of Gal. 5:22–23 is the list of the works of the flesh (5:19–21) that result when Christians leave the love and the Spirit of Christ and pervert liberty into license. The general context of 1 Corinthians 13, reaching as far back as the first chapter (see, e.g., 1:10–13; 3:1–4; 4:6–7, 18–21; 5:1–5; 6:1–11; 8:1–3; 10:1–13; 11:17–22; 12:1–3, 14–26), depicts the works of the flesh practiced at Corinth. Second, 1 Corinthians 13 deals with the same realities as Gal. 5:22–23: in Galatians, Paul employs nouns; in Corinthians, verbs related to those nouns, with love as the subject. Thus, in 1 Cor. 13:4–7, Paul writes, "Love is patient and kind . . . ; it does not rejoice at wrong, but rejoices in the right. . . . Love bears all things, believes all things, hopes all things, endures all things."

The fact that the word "fruit" is chosen by Paul in Galatians may well point to the fact that he thinks of Christians as a living, growing, producing organism (see 1 Cor. 12:12–30, on Christ's body, the church). Further, much has properly been made of the fact that Paul speaks of "fruit," not "fruits," and that love is named first: Paul might have stopped with love as the fruit of the Spirit, implying that the remainder of the cluster is included in love, which 1 Corinthians makes explicit. In the light of Gal. 5:22–23 and 1 Corinthians 13, we proceed with eyes on Jesus, the incarnation of God's love.

Love. If there was one impression that Jesus made on the lowly people with whom he spent most of his time, it was that "Jesus really cares about me." "The disciple whom Jesus loved" was not one loved exclusively; there is no one Jesus did not, does not, love. And whenever God's love in Christ is mentioned, it is implicitly or openly associated with Jesus' death. ". . . who loved me and gave himself for me" (Gal. 2:20), writes Paul of the Son of God who has captured his faith. The last book in the Bible doxologizes Jesus Christ the faithful witness: "To him who loves us and has freed us from our sins by his blood . . . to him be glory" (Rev. 1:5–6). The seer has a vision of final victory when our brothers and sisters will have conquered Satan "by the blood of the Lamb and by the word of their testimony, for they loved not their lives even unto death" (12:11). For the disciple as for the Master, the way to victory is the way of the cross.

Joy. "A man of sorrows and acquainted with grief," was Jesus a man of joy also? There is much evidence that Jesus is "joy of man's desiring," that he gives others profound joy. But does he himself rejoice? There are clues that he does.

According to the Epistle to the Hebrews, Christ came into the world saying, "Lo, I have come to do thy will, O God" (10:7). Jesus' ruling passion was to do his Father's will, and for this he could sometimes ignore even eating: "I have food to eat which you do not know. . . . My food is to do the will of him who sent me, and to accomplish his

work." Jesus was one of the sowers and reapers who rejoiced together
near fields white for the harvest while the Samaritan woman was
sowing in Sychar (John 4:31–36). Jesus rejoiced in doing God's will.

Later in John, Jesus spoke of his joy in a context that further interprets its nature: "If you keep my commandments, you will abide in my
love. . . . These things I have spoken to you, that my joy may be in you,
and that your joy may be full" (15:10–11). Jesus would mediate for his
disciples his joy of abiding in his Father and his love while keeping his
commandments. In Jesus' "high-priestly prayer" he again shows concern that his joy may be fulfilled in his disciples, a joy involving their
oneness in a hostile world (John 17:13–14).

There is a less somber aspect to the joy of Jesus during his earthly
life. Luke 15, a chapter of joy, is alive with significant clues. Repeated
is the emphasis on the joy in heaven over one sinner who repents. If
there is joy in heaven over a single sinner repenting, there is joy in Jesus
as he "welcomes sinners and feasts with them." These include a
"woman of the city, who was a sinner," whose faith saved her; Zacchaeus of Jericho, to whose house salvation came when Jesus invited
himself in; and others named and not named in Scripture. Jesus' joy
in welcoming sinners is of course closely related to his joy in doing his
Father's will; it is a rejoicing at the results of his and the Father's
mission.

Paul in prison caught the spirit of Jesus' joy accurately while
encouraging the Philippians: "Rejoice in the Lord always; again I will
say, Rejoice" (4:4). For neither Paul nor the persecuted Philippians did
joy come cheap; it was irrepressible simply because rooted in him
"who for the joy that was set before him endured the cross, despising
the shame" (Heb. 12:2). All this is reminiscent of those other early disciples who, beaten at Jerusalem and charged to quit speaking in Jesus'
name, "left the presence of the council, rejoicing that they were
counted worthy to suffer dishonor for the name" and "did not cease
teaching and preaching Jesus as the Christ" (Acts 5:41–42).

Peace. Of Jesus as a youth we read, "And Jesus increased in wisdom
and stature, and in favor with God and man" (Luke 2:52). We have no
reason to think he did not "seek peace and pursue it" among his family
and townspeople. In his public ministry, however, that he might be in
his Father's will, the Son of man found himself at odds with his own
family and an antagonist of Jew and Roman. The peace he knew and

gives is compatible with tribulation. He could even say, "I have not come to bring peace, but a sword" (Matt. 10:34).

A rather simple man fled from a congregational meeting one night greatly agitated. Asked why, he replied, "The janitor and the trustees are arguing about those cemetery lots. I believe there's going to be bloodshed, so I got out!"

Christ's apostles knew, and we know, that when people "justified by faith have peace with God" (Rom. 5:1), they have found the "more excellent way." It is this kind of peace which is primarily in Paul's mind as he writes, "The fruit of the Spirit is love, joy, peace." Paul writes the Romans that the kingdom of God does not mean arguing about food and drink; rather it is "righteousness and peace and joy in the Holy Spirit. . . . Let us then pursue what makes for peace and for mutual upbuilding" (14:17-19). Christ is searching out and raising up in our congregations people who wage peace, blessed peacemakers. How about a secretary of peace in the cabinet of our nation's president?

Patience and kindness. "Love is patient and kind." The picture behind "to be patient" is of a God who delays the breaking-forth of his wrath; it will erupt. When people do not acknowledge God as God, he gives them over to perverted passions and death-deserving devilry of all kinds, as Paul teaches in Romans 1. And God's judgment hangs ominously over not only those who do such things but also those who approve of those who practice them, so promoting sin. But for God to give people up to a base mind and improper conduct is a case of "being cruel to be kind." God wants people to repent. Paul therefore goes on, "Or do you presume upon the riches of his kindness and forbearance and patience? Do you not know that God's kindness is meant to lead you to repentance? But by your hard and impenitent heart you are storing up wrath for yourself" (Rom. 2:4-5). God is so patient and kind that a just wrath is long stayed. God's anger has a long, long fuse; God's kindness waits and waits and waits for hard and impenitent hearts to repent and defuse his righteous anger. One who has experienced God's patience and kindness is patient and kind, by the Spirit.

Goodness. "The fruit of the Spirit . . . is patience, kindness, goodness." Strictly speaking, "no one is good but God alone." In contexts such as this, there is a rather austere connotation to the terms "good" and "goodness." Kindness is God's goodness reaching out in love for the undeserving; "he is kind to the ungrateful and to the selfish." God's goodness rightfully does its "strange work" of calling people to task for their sin. And in kindness, God's goodness does its "proper work" of trying to bring people to repent.

With God's revelation in the life, death, and resurrection of Christ, the people of God were given the possibility of being transformed so as "to prove what is the will of God, what is good and acceptable and perfect." Paul meaningfully, therefore, encourages the Thessalonians, "See that none of you repays evil for evil, but always seek to do good to one another and to all" (1 Thess. 5:15).

Faithfulness. The Greek word for "faithfulness" here, *pistis,* is the same word that in so many Pauline passages means "faith" or "trust." But in this context, it is, like the other words in the list, directed to human relationships; therefore it is accurately translated as "faithfulness."

In a vision of heaven opened, the author of the Book of Revelation sees a white horse. "He who sat upon it is called Faithful and True" (19:11). His Father is characterized in like manner by God's people of old and of today. In Psalm 136, a single refrain occurs twenty-six times; it must make a statement of extraordinary significance to God's worshiping congregation! The refrain: ". . . for his steadfast love endures for ever." Jesus loved his disciples to the end. In 1 Corinthians 13, Paul does not say, "Love is faithful," in so many words, but he does state it in various ways: "Love never ends," and "Love abides."

Gentleness. Gentleness is directly related to the way Jesus characterizes himself in his well-known invitation at the end of Matthew 11: "Come to me, all who labor and are heavy laden, and I will give you rest. Take my yoke upon you, and learn from me; for I am gentle and lowly in heart, and you will find rest for your souls. For my yoke is easy, and my burden is light." He invites the burdened to learn from him gentleness. His yoke is easy, fashioned precisely for its purpose, since Jesus knows what it is to be a human being and what it is to suffer. Therefore he does not offer to remove all burdens but to give a yoke custom-made in order that burdens may be borne with inner serenity. On Palm Sunday he comes not as a political Messiah but as a "king . . . gentle and riding on an ass." Since the gentle shall inherit the earth, he pronounces them blessed; they are heirs by faith to the "promise to Abraham and his descendants, that they should inherit the world" (Rom. 4:13). In the very context of Gal. 5:23, Paul gives us an insight into what he means by gentleness. "Brethren," he writes, "if a man is overtaken in any trespass, you who are spiritual should restore him in a spirit of gentleness. Look to yourself, lest you too be tempted" (Gal. 6:1). Gently Paul initiates this counsel while "putting the best construction" on such a possible situation; and all the action is toward *restoring* the one overtaken, "in a spirit of gentleness."

In considering Jesus, Stephen, Paul, and others, it becomes obvious that gentleness is perfectly compatible with the iron will of one whose joy lies in obeying God, not people, and whose actions and speech are therefore sometimes jarring in order to be gentle. The same Jesus who pronounces the seven woes on the scribes and the Pharisees weeps heartbroken over the city, "O Jerusalem, Jerusalem . . ."

Self-control. Self-control is the ninth and last fruit of the Spirit in Paul's list, a list not meant to be exhaustive, yet which is significant and suggestive. Self-control is perhaps a stronger reminder than the others that Paul writes of the fruit of the Spirit in a context of their opposites and counterfeits in the immediately preceding verses. The works of the flesh recorded there conclude with "drunkenness, carousing, and the like." Drunkenness and carousing seem to be placed in the final position in order to show their diametrical opposition to self-control. Jesus occasionally enjoyed good food and drink and was slanderously labeled a glutton and a drunkard. He who in his person embodied and brought God's kingly rule to humankind surely did not act in such a manner as to forfeit the kingdom of God (Gal. 5:21). Since their earliest days, Christ's people have been convinced that he is "one who in every respect has been tempted as we are, yet without sinning." Just as Jesus exercised self-control, his Spirit grows that versatile fruit in the believer.

Spirit versus Flesh:
A Deadly Duel

Fruit is not produced by a dead trunk fertilized by the law; fruit grows when faith, a new creation (see Gal. 5:6; 6:17), is planted into Christ by gospel, Spirit, baptism. "Now that faith has come, we are no longer under a custodian; for in Christ Jesus you are all sons of God, through faith. For as many of you as were baptized into Christ have put on Christ" (Gal. 3:25–27). Once the Spirit of Christ dwells in one through faith, fruit is produced—unless the believer perverts freedom into an opportunity for the flesh (Gal. 5:13). Before the Spirit comes through faith, there is no contest: the anti-God flesh, totally in control, grinds out works of the flesh and is doomed not to inherit God's rule. But when the Spirit brings a person to faith, there ensues a duel to the death between Christ's Spirit and the believer's flesh. "For the desires of the flesh are against the Spirit, and the desires of the Spirit are against the flesh; for these are opposed to each other, to prevent you from doing what you would. But if you are led by the Spirit you are not under the law" (Gal. 5:17–18). As Paul writes in Romans, "If you live according to the flesh you will die, but if by the Spirit you put to death the deeds of the body you will live" (8:13). The alternatives are death and life.

Spiritual fruit is inevitable, but the believer is responsible. In the life in the Spirit there are pitfalls. One such might be called a complacent fatalism that says, "Well, if fruit is the product of the Spirit, I have no responsibility. Let it produce." Such a philosophy is un-Christian if Paul is Christian. He vigorously exhorts his congregations to act decisively, precisely because God is at work in them "both to will and to work for his good pleasure" (Phil. 2:12–13). Of Jesus "in the days of his flesh," the author of Hebrews writes, "Although he was a Son, he learned obedience through what he suffered" (5:8). Through his suffering in Gethsemane and elsewhere, Jesus learned obedience by trustfully obeying his Father. If the one true man had to learn obedience, it will not come automatically to the rest of humankind either.

According to Jesus' life and words, being his disciple is taking up a cross and following him. Being with him reveals ever more deeply "that nothing good dwells within me, that is, in my flesh." There are powerful forces ever trying to enslave the believer in this earthly existence, but slavery need not result, because "there is no condemnation for those in Christ Jesus." "Sin will have no dominion over you, since you are not under law but under grace" (Rom. 7:18; 8:1; 6:14).

It is the gospel of the cross that mediates Christ's Spirit, the Spirit who produces his fruit. Therefore Paul begins 1 Corinthians with a reminder that *he* was not crucified for them, *Christ* was. Neither were they baptized in Paul's name, but in Christ's. He continues with a concentration on the "cross of Christ," on the "word of the cross," on "Jesus Christ and him crucified." Although Paul yields to no one in his insistence on the life-giving and life-sustaining significance of baptism and the Lord's Supper, he warns that most of "our fathers [who] were all baptized into Moses . . . and drank from . . . Christ . . . nevertheless . . . were overthrown in the wilderness" (1 Cor. 10:1–5). But "God is faithful" and will provide you an escape route from any temptation (1 Cor. 10:13).

When God's Spirit reveals to his people what has happened in Christ Jesus, they will better understand that the Spirit's fruit is not merely possible but inevitable—unless they are dead or dying.

Jesus has come with power and will come with glory. What happened when Jesus died, rose, and ascended? Did God's kingdom, God's reign, vanish from the earth? God forbid! During his earthly life, Jesus made some very puzzling predictions that may portend the coming of an *intermediate* stage of God's kingly rule. After his clarion call to self-denying, cross-bearing discipleship, Jesus said, "Truly, there are some standing here who will not taste death before they see the kingdom of God come with power" (Mark 9:1). After his resurrection, when he was commissioning his disciples who had "disbelieved for joy," Jesus said, "You are witnesses of these things. And behold, I send the promise of my Father upon you; but stay in the city, until you are clothed with power from on high" (Luke 24:48–49).

In Luke's second volume the disciples asked Jesus after the resurrection, "Lord, will you at this time restore the kingdom to Israel?" (Acts 1:6). Evidently they still misunderstood the kingdom in terms of a secular state, but Jesus enlightened them saying, "It is not for you to know times or seasons. . . . But you shall receive power when the Holy Spirit has come upon you; and you shall be my witnesses in Jerusalem and in all Judea and Samaria and to the end of the earth" (1:7–8; note the word "power" in Mark, Luke, and Acts above, and cf. Rom. 1:4).

It seems that some of Jesus' listeners understood his predictions in too narrow a way; they thought he was coming again gloriously to consummate all history before the end of their own generation. But his words are open to a more plausible interpretation. Did not the kingdom of God come with *power* in the death, resurrection, and ascension of Jesus and his sending of the Holy Spirit? When the Word became "frail flesh," he was weak, vulnerable, subject to the kind of existence we know. But his death, resurrection, ascension, and return in the Spirit are, through the gospel, the "power of God for salvation." "For the word of the cross is folly to those who are perishing, but to us who are being saved it is the power of God" (1 Cor. 1:18). The Word incarnate has not deserted this planet, leaving us orphans; he is here in *power* in his Spirit. Truly, the rule of God did come with power during the lives of some of Jesus' first-century contemporaries; God's rule with power is still among us, as God changes people and destinies by his Word and Sacraments. What greater power is there than Jesus in his Word? Jesus was his own style of Messiah, the Suffering Servant, and he tried to teach his disciples that to come with power his kingdom did not need to outdo the northern lights! There are two interpretations of the coming of God's kingdom that are in harmony with the possibility presented here—one from the early church, the other from Luther.

There is a fascinating alternate textual reading of the second petition of the Lord's Prayer in Luke 11:2, which instead of saying, "Thy kingdom come," goes, "Thy Holy Spirit come upon us and cleanse us." Although it is very likely not the original text, it at least indicates what some early Christians thought was involved in "Thy kingdom come." Then in Luther's Small Catechism, under "The Second Petition," there is a remarkable explanation of when God's kingdom comes to us: "God's kingdom comes when our heavenly Father gives us his Holy Spirit, so that by his grace we believe his holy Word and live a godly life on earth now and in heaven forever."

Luther's words remind us that the coming of God's kingdom in power through his Spirit in his Word by no means exhausts the coming of his reign. At the consummation of history, he who is King of kings and Lord of lords will come in glory and every knee will bow "and every tongue confess that Jesus Christ is Lord, to the glory of God the Father" (Phil. 2:10–11).

7

Charismatic Christians
Use Their Gifts

To remember who they are. When Satan attacked Luther, he counterattacked in potent Latin, "Baptizatus sum!" meaning, "I have been baptized! God has baptized me—he is faithful!"

In the Small Catechism, Luther joins being baptized and saved with believing. Baptism "gives everlasting salvation to all who believe." Then he quotes Mark 16:16: "He who believes and is baptized will be saved; but he who does not believe will be condemned." One can be baptized and not believe, and be condemned. "Just because everyone in Saxony is baptized," says Luther, "does not mean everyone in Saxony is a Christian. Of course it happens that many leap overboard into the sea and perish."[29]

Baptized believers need to keep hearing the promises of the gospel that create and re-create their trust in Christ into whom they are baptized. Mere exhortation is impotent to maintain faith. Indispensable, as C. F. W. Walther insists, is "preaching faith into a person's heart by laying the Gospel promises before him."[30]

To present their total selves to God. To Christians at Rome, baptized believers, Paul writes, "I appeal to you, therefore, brothers and sisters, through the mercies of God to present your bodies a living sacrifice, holy, acceptable to God, your appropriate service. And do not be conformed to this age, but be transformed by the renewal of your mind so as to prove what the will of God is, good and acceptable and perfect" (Rom. 12:1–2, au. trans.). The day of dead animal sacrifices is over, the time for living human sacrifices is here, "through God's mercies."

We present our total selves to God because in Christ he has presented his total self to us, for us. The ways God draws believers into being living sacrifices are commensurate with his unlimited grace and the vast differences among believers and churches. Suffering deepens some, ecstasy *and* agony others, or slow growth. Some are set afire by Bible studies as modern as tomorrow. Others serve and are served by the Christ in visiting food shelves, clothes closets, and day-care and night shelters. "Service evangelism" ministers to whole persons, serving and served.[31]

During the seventies the Lutheran churches in the United States removed two and one-half million members from their rolls. Could much of this huge loss be traced back to a lack of challenge to baptized believers to rededicate themselves totally to God through God's mercies?

To shape up for finding God's will. "Do not keep being conformed to this age," writes Paul after his appeal to Christians at Rome to present their total selves to God. Our old nature battles to keep us shaped to the "now" age, not without some success. But God's Spirit has plans far different.

"But keep being transformed by the renewal of your mind," continues Paul. God's Spirit counterattacks the old nature in baptized believers and is daily transforming them in order that "Christ be formed in them." "And we all, with unveiled face, beholding the glory of the Lord, are being changed into his likeness from one degree of glory to another" (2 Cor. 3:18). In faith, we accept what Paul writes in spite of much evidence to the contrary.

Why all this shaping up? "That you may prove by testing what the good and acceptable and perfect will of God is," writes Paul. When you attempt to discern God's will for yourself and others, a certain modesty is becoming. The Bible abounds with believers who learned by trial and error while being transformed. We too "walk by faith, not by sight."

To discover and affirm their gifts. A group of lay women had been studying Acts and the spread of the gospel in the mission of the early church. The leader then asked, "How do we carry on this mission in our congregation?" Before the session ended, each participant was requested to think of one gift she had been given to exercise in the church's work. "I'll begin by sharing one that challenges me," the leader volunteered. "I like to organize and carry through with my plans and those that others suggest. I feel good about helping make things happen." Within a few minutes many gifts had been revealed, pointed out, and evoked: serving, worshiping, teaching, sharing, befriending teenagers and the handicapped, intercessory praying and entertaining the lonely. There is something festive and creative about simply being Christian human beings together, better to understand others and how we ourselves are being perceived, "for the common good."

As a part of his counsel, the author of the Letter to the Ephesians writes, "And do not get drunk with wine, for that is debauchery; but be filled with the Spirit, addressing one another in psalms and hymns and spiritual songs, singing and making melody to the Lord with all your heart, always and for everything giving thanks in the name of our Lord Jesus Christ to God our Father" (5:18–20). Life-illuminating meaning is a gift God makes to church members assembled for worship as they musically address one another, heartily thanking and praising the Lord. What other corporate gifts may a congregation have and exercise? Location, constituency, means, pastor, an inventory, prayer, openness, investigation, brainstorming, conferring with neighboring parishes as well as district and synodical headquarters—one or a number of these may help a congregation as a whole discover its particular genius and mission and perform accordingly.

For evangelical outreach. The church that is not reaching out is a corpse or about to be. A church *is* mission, commissioned to claim God's turf for Jesus Christ, Lord.

Reaching-out is happening in Our Savior Luther Church, of Hartland, Wisconsin, because members are reaching in through Bible study. "It is bringing in other people," says Barbara Foss.[32]

When Buddhists moved in next door to a church across from the capitol in St. Paul, Minnesota, the members took a plunge. About half the two hundred worshipers on a typical Sunday are now Asian and "we're struggling way over our head." Sometimes when gifts of grace are desperately needed, they are lavishly granted and zestfully employed, with a metropolitan impact.[33] Many congregations are "struggling way over their heads"—which is risky but exhilarating.

This ministry in St. Paul is growing. "Our two youth choirs are all

Cambodian and Hmong kids," says the pastor. "If we can be open to each other, regardless of our color, or race, or background—that's what we really want to work at."

To witness for Christ. Lest "sawdust trails," "doorbelling," or any other stereotypes of evangelism leap to mind in connection with witnessing, consider Edward F. Markquart's succinct definition: "Rather, intentional witnessing helps people verbalize the faith within already existing natural relationships." On the basis of questionnaires, it is estimated that seventy-five to eighty percent of those who begin to worship Christ in church are brought by friends or relatives.[34] Such witnessing works, in congregation and synod.[35]

Late one evening a neighbor phoned a Christian couple, asking them to come over for coffee and conversation. Though reluctant to leave their children, the couple were urged by their older daughter to go; she would "hold the fort." Arriving next door, they found Miriam, the young wife and mother, distraught. She had been seeing a psychiatrist regularly and had been calling in a priest and getting outside help with the housework. For hours, the woman told her story to her husband and the two neighbors: where she had been, where she was. The others mostly listened, but God's story began to be told, in segments, by the visitors. Hours into the next morning, Miriam turned to the man next door, burned her eyes into his and demanded, "Do you really believe in this forgiving Jesus you've been telling me about? Do you really trust him?"

"Yes," was the quiet, firm reply. Through her story, God's story, and the couple's story, the Holy Spirit evidently did something that night. The woman was able to give up her psychiatrist and her cleaning woman, and she faced life with courage. Some two decades later these two couples, although twelve thousand miles apart, are close because of that watershed evening. Whenever they meet, there is communication that swiftly goes deep. Through God's story and through listening and responding, a miracle may happen; it may not.

The invitation may have seemed casual, but it was far from careless; rather, it was given after considerable deliberation, with a prayer that the time was right. It was added as a postscript to a business letter to Helen, an acquaintance of several months. Helen was a single parent living in the area with her two daughters, and she had previously been invited by John and Mary to an orchestra concert in their church. John and Mary had not seen her there, though they had looked for her diligently.

P.S. Wonder if you got to that orchestra concert at the church that night . . . ; you know all three of you are very welcome there, any time. We'd be glad to take you there, but you may already have a church home or prefer not to attend a church. John and Mary.

Dear Friends John and Mary,
. . . I did attend the orchestra concert and enjoyed it very much. I also would appreciate attending church with you both. I believe it would be good for Joan to start regular Sunday-school classes. Could you call and let me know the time of the services? I would be delighted to attend with you.

Sincerely,
Helen Cartier

Within a few months Helen and Joan were part of a network of Christian friends in the congregation. The older daughter attended services only occasionally, but she was a definite part of the circle of concerned people and was responding very positively.

All Christians are charismatic. Dear Christian reader, you are charismatic. You are a distinctive creation of God. For you the Son of God died. You have been re-created in Christ Jesus for your special ministry in the particular congregation and community where you have been placed. "Having gifts that differ according to the grace given to us," let us do our best to use them all.

Notes

1. Hubert H. Humphrey, as quoted in *Time,* January 23, 1978, 25.

2. Oscar Cullmann, *Baptism in the New Testament* (Chicago: Alec R. Allenson, 1956), 78.

3. Larry Christenson, *The Charismatic Renewal among Lutherans* (Minneapolis: Lutheran Charismatic Renewal Services, 1976), 66.

4. Michael Green, *I Believe in the Holy Spirit* (Grand Rapids: Wm. B. Eerdmans, 1975), 196.

5. Hans Küng, *The Church* (New York: Sheed & Ward, 1967), 187.

6. Ernst Käsemann, *Essays on New Testament Themes* (London: SCM Press, 1971), 73.

7. G. Friedrich, in *Theological Dictionary of the New Testament (TDNT),* ed., G. Friedrich (Grand Rapids: Wm. B. Eerdmans, 1968), 6:848.

8. Green, *Holy Spirit,* 171–72.

9. For a fine, succinct discussion of Montanism, see Jaroslav Pelikan, *The Christian Tradition,* vol. 1, *The Emergence of the Catholic Tradition* (Chicago: Univ. of Chicago Press, 1971), 97–108.

10. Arthur Montgomery, in *Seeds of Fire* (Minneapolis: Division for Life and Mission in the Congregation, ALC, 1984), 2:3–4.

11. Otto Schmitz, in *TDNT* 5:799.

12. Rudolf Bultmann, in *TDNT* 1:707–8.

13. Ibid., 708–9.

14. Krister Stendahl, *Paul among Jews and Gentiles* (Philadelphia: Fortress Press, 1976), 115–16.

15. Felicitas Goodman, "A Study of Tongues," *Event,* November/December 1973, 28.

16. Ibid., 27–28.

17. See Kilian McDonnell, "The Hunger for God," *Event,* November/December 1973, 21.

18. Stendahl, *Paul among Jews and Gentiles,* 121–23.

19. Ibid., 123–24.

20. H. Beyer, in *TDNT* 2:87.

21. Ibid.

22. Natalie Zett, in *Seeds of Fire* 2:7–8.

23. Stendahl, *Paul among Jews and Gentiles,* 56.

24. Jennifer N. Peterson, "Where There's No Limit," *Lutheran Standard* 24/15 (September 21, 1984): 12–14.

25. Bo Reicke, in *TDNT* 6:701.

26. Arthur Montgomery, in *Seeds of Fire* 1:8–9.

27. W. Grundmann, in *TDNT* 2:303.

28. *Constitution and Rules of the World Council of Churches* (London: Billing & Son, 1961), 3. Emphasis mine.

29. Martin Luther, "The Babylonian Captivity of the Church," in *Luther's Works,* vol. 36, ed. Abdel R. Wentz (Philadelphia: Fortress Press, 1959), 61.

30. C. Walther, *The Proper Distinction between Law and Gospel,* trans. W. H. T. Dau (St. Louis: Concordia Pub. House, 1929), 351.

31. Richard S. Armstrong, *Service Evangelism* (Philadelphia: Westminster Press, 1979).

32. Montgomery, in *Seeds of Fire* 1:14–15.

33. Ibid. 2:13–14.

34. Edward F. Markquart, *Witnesses for Christ: Training for Intentional Witnessing, Leader's Guide* (Minneapolis: Augsburg Pub. House, 1981), 3, 14.

35. Floramae Geiser, "Making Outreach No. 1: A Michigan Program Puts Evangelism in the Driver's Seat," *Lutheran* 25/10 (May 20, 1987): 8–9.

For Further Reading

Andrews, E. "Spiritual Gifts." In *Interpreter's Dictionary of the Bible (IDB)*, 435–37. Nashville: Abingdon Press, 1962. Gifts are defined and evaluated, with emphasis on the gift that is the Spirit and on the centrality of love. There is a bibliography of older works.

Ellis, E. E. "Spiritual Gifts." In *IDB* Sup, 841–42. Nashville: Abingdon Press, 1976. *The* gift from the risen Lord is seen to be the Holy Spirit enabling the confession "Jesus is Lord." Ellis develops the idea that, while gifts may be sought, the sovereign Spirit gives as the Spirit wills for the church's good. "Baptism in the Spirit," fruit and gifts, and distinctions among ministries are treated. There is a useful bibliography.

Furnish, V. P. "Spiritual Gifts." In *Harper's Bible Dictionary*, 989–90. San Francisco: Harper & Row, 1985. This is a carefully crafted article, comprehensive in spite of its brevity. Distinguished from the fruit of the Spirit, the gifts are grouped under utterance, practical ministry, and wonderworking faith. Scripture is cited with masterly skill; authentic insights abound.

Koenig, John. *Charismata: God's Gifts for God's People*. Philadelphia: Westminster Press, 1978. This is probably the best all-around book on the subject. Excellent scholarship is evident throughout, empathic, incisive. Giftedness in Old Testament and New is treated, and how the Giver renews and deploys the gifted. The gift of the cross is squarely faced; contemporary theologies are candidly evaluated. In command of his field, the author brings a salutary up-to-date perspective.

Opsahl, P. D., ed. *The Holy Spirit in the Life of the Church: From Biblical Times to the Present*, 10–98. Minneapolis: Augsburg Pub. House, 1978. This volume grew out of a study project conducted by the Division of Theological Studies of the Lutheran Council in the U.S.A. It is packed with significant, sophisticated materials, the result of prepared papers delivered at four conferences, each involving twenty to twenty-five pastors and theological professors, some of whom are neo-Pentecostals. Most of the papers commissioned for this study are printed in revised form. The pages designated deal with the Spirit in the Old Testament, the Synoptics, and Acts (G. Krodel), the Spirit in Paul and John (E. Krentz), and the Spirit in the patristic and medieval church (W. Rusch). Five other excellent chapters and two appendixes make this a gold mine of relevant information for today's churches.

Schweizer, Eduard. *The Holy Spirit*. Philadelphia: Fortress Press, 1980. For a concise yet comprehensive presentation of biblical teaching on the nature and work of the Holy Spirit, this book is excellent, probably the best; it is erudite in nontechnical language. After surveying some past and current views on the Spirit, the author presents three chapters treating the evidence from the Old Testament, from intertestamental Judaism, and from the New Testament. The final chapter deals with various accents regarding the Spirit in the New Testament and concludes with the marks of the Spirit.